New Mermaids

General editor: Brian Gibbons
Professor of English Literature, University of Münster

New Mermaids

The Alchemist

All for Love

Arden of Faversham

Bartholmew Fair

The Beaux' Stratagem

The Changeling

A Chaste Maid in Cheapside

The Country Wife

The Critic

Dr Faustus

The Duchess of Malfi

The Dutch Courtesan

Eastward Ho!

Edward the Second

Epicoene or The Silent Woman

Every Man In His Humour

Gammer Gurton's Needle

An Ideal Husband

The Importance of Being Earnest

The Jew of Malta

The Knight of the Burning Pestle

Lady Windermere's Fan

Love for Love

The Malcontent

The Man of Mode

Marriage A-la-Mode

A New Way to Pay Old Debts

The Old Wife's Tale

The Playboy of the Western
    World

The Provoked Wife

The Recruiting Officer

The Relapse

The Revenger's Tragedy

The Rivals

The Roaring Girl

The Rover

The School for Scandal

She Stoops to Conquer

The Shoemaker's Holiday

The Spanish Tragedy

Tamburlaine

Three Late Medieval Morality
    Plays
  Mankind
  Everyman
  Mundus et Infans

'Tis Pity She's a Whore

Volpone

The Way of the World

The White Devil

The Witch

The Witch of Edmonton

A Woman Killed with Kindness

A Woman of No Importance

Women Beware Women

New Mermaids

RICHARD BRINSLEY SHERIDAN

The Rivals

Edited by Tiffany Stern

Senior Lecturer in English, Oxford Brookes University

A & C BLACK • LONDON
W W NORTON • NEW YORK

Second edition 2004
A & C Black Publishers Limited
37 Soho Square, London WID 3QZ
www.acblack.com

ISBN 0–7136–6765–6

First New Mermaid edition 1979 by Ernest Benn Limited

Published in the United States of America by
W. W. Norton & Company Inc.
500 Fifth Avenue, New York, N.Y. 10110

ISBN 0–393–92752–0

A CIP catalogue record for this book
is available from the British Library

Printed in Great Britain by
Bookmarque Ltd, Croydon, Surrey

CONTENTS

Acknowledgements   vi

Introduction

SUMMARY   1

GENRE   1

STRUCTURE   4

THEMES   7

CHARACTERS: WOMEN   11

CHARACTERS: MEN   12

DATE AND HISTORICAL CONTEXT   16

RECENT STAGE HISTORY   19

NOTE ON THE TEXT   22

SOURCES   23

AUTHOR   25

Further Reading   28

The Rivals   31

Preface   33

Prologue   38

Prologue Spoken on the Tenth Night   41

Dramatis Personae   43

The Play   45

Epilogue   170

Appendix : Larpent Variations   173

ACKNOWLEDGEMENTS

My first and greatest debt is to previous editors of *The Rivals*, especially
Cecil Price and Michael Cordner. I am also grateful to the many
tremendous commentators who have written about this play. They can be
found in footnotes and bibliography. My work has been supported by the
staffs of the Bodleian library and the Cambridge University Library; I am
particularly indebted to the staff of Huntington library where the Larpent
manuscript is housed. Oxford Brookes generously gave me sabbatical leave
in which to complete this project; I spent that time at Clare Hall, Cambridge,
where the master and fellows had kindly granted me a fellowship: my thanks
to both. In Cambridge, Kate Bennett conversed with me about comedies,
and Jocelyn Harris shared with me her expertise on eighteenth-century
Bath, and saved me many months' work: her help has been invaluable. The
assistance of John Jowett and Gordon McMullan has improved this edition
in countless ways; I have constantly benefitted from the textual advice of
Brian and Sue Gibbons; and friends and family for whom my love will never
be miscellaneous helped me crack obscure malapropisms: Peter Holbrook,
Elspeth Jajdelska, Wojtek Jajdelski, Gareth Mann, Elisabeth Stern and
Geoffrey Stern. Huge thanks to them and to my flatmates, Alastair Blanshard,
Michael Brett, Max Liebermann, and Tracey Sowerby, who lived long with
The Rivals and who even performed sections of the play at our Christmas
party.

INTRODUCTION

SUMMARY

Lydia Languish, whose view on life is shaped entirely by the romantic novels she reads, has fallen in love with a penniless soldier, Ensign Beverley. But Beverley is in fact Captain Jack Absolute, the son of a baronet, who has disguised himself to fulfil Lydia's desires for an impoverished romantic hero. Enraged at the attachment, Lydia's aunt, the 'queen of the dictionary', Mrs Malaprop, has arranged a match between her niece and the son of Sir Anthony Absolute – Captain Jack Absolute. Jack is thus his own rival.

Lydia's other suitors are a country bumpkin, Bob Acres, who has come to Bath to learn sophisticated ways, and Sir Lucius O'Trigger, a belligerent Irishman. Sir Lucius believes himself to be wooing Lydia by letter; in fact the woman writing to him under the name of 'Delia' is the lovelorn Mrs Malaprop.

Sir Anthony's ward, Julia Melville, is also in Bath, as is her fiancé Faulkland. Julia is constant in her love; Faulkland is racked by doubts: does Julia love him or the fact that he once saved her life? He continually tests Julia's love, to the point where she finally severs their engagement.

Jack reveals his true identity to Lydia who, incensed that she has been fooled by the man she loved, renounces her attachment. Leaving Lydia's house in a rage, Jack meets Sir Lucius, who is spoiling for a fight, and accepts his challenge to a duel. Meanwhile, Lydia's other scorned suitor, Bob Acres, sends a challenge to 'Beverley'; Jack now has to fight on two counts – and under two names – for the woman who has rejected him.

Jack, Sir Lucius and Acres arrive at Kingsmead Fields to fight their respective duels. Faulkland, who has come as Jack's second, is mistaken for 'Beverley'. Word of the intended contests reaches Sir Anthony and the ladies, who rush to the battleground to stop the bloodshed. Their arrival brings about a scene of revelation in which Jack confesses that he is Beverley and Mrs Malaprop reveals that she is Delia. Sir Lucius and Acres drop their claims on Lydia; Sir Lucius also rejects Mrs Malaprop. Lydia, realising she still loves Jack, asks for his forgiveness and hand in marriage; Julia forgives Faulkland and agrees to marry him. The assembled company are invited by Acres to the New Rooms for a celebration of the prospective weddings.

GENRE

With its advice on contemporary wig-wearing habits and its references to buildings recently erected in Bath, *The Rivals* is undoubtedly set in the England of the late eighteenth century. Nevertheless it lacks the straightforward sentimentality of other plays written around the same time, like Hugh Kelly's popular *False Delicacy* (1768). *The Rivals* resembles Restoration plays (written some hundred years earlier); indeed Sheridan was called by his contemporaries 'the Congreve of the present theatre'.[1] But though the witty repartee of *The Rivals* is reminiscent of the writing of William Congreve (1670–1729), the whimsicality, charity and moral tone are not. Indeed Sheridan was given the job of modifying Congreve for eighteenth-century performance, 'retrenching some licentious expressions' in *The Old Batchelor, Love for Love*, and *The Way of the World*, for an audience 'whose ears are become exceedingly chaste': Sheridan was Congreve without the bitterness, the bullish sexuality, the acerbic edge.

While revising Congreve's plays, Sheridan further changed their natures by 'connecting . . . character and sentiment' in a manner that pleased eighteenth-century spectators.[2] And yet in his writings Sheridan continually inveighed against sentimentality, linking himself to the dramatist Oliver Goldsmith (1730?–1774) whose *Comparison Between Laughing and Sentimental Comedy* (1773) set the agenda for antisentimentalists:

> in [sentimental comedies] almost all the Characters are good, and exceedingly generous; . . . though they want Humour, [they] have abundance of Sentiment and Feeling. If they happen to have Faults or Foibles, the Spectator is taught . . . to applaud them, in consideration of the goodness of their hearts; so that Folly, instead of being ridiculed, is commended.[3]

Goldsmith wrote a play, *She Stoops to Conquer* (performed in 1773), as a prototype of 'laughing' rather than sentimental comedy. *The Rivals* claims to be another play written in the same mode; its tenth night prologue condemns the chaste primness of the 'sentimental muse' (23) and promotes instead the humour and invention of 'pure' comedy.

Yet though Sheridan regularly derided sentimental comedies, he added sentiment to Congreve's writing, and gave *The Rivals* a highly sentimental subplot.[4] Indeed, *The Rivals* only escaped utter damnation in its first

---

[1] David Erskine Baker, *Biographia Dramatica* (1782), p. 417.

[2] Thomas Davies, *Life of David Garrick*, 2 vols (1780), II, 244.

[3] Oliver Goldsmith, *An Essay on the Theatre; or, a Comparison between Laughing and Sentimental Comedy* (1773), in *Collected Works*, ed. Arthur Friedman, 5 vols (Oxford, 1966), III, 212.

[4] Sheridan inveighed against sentimental comedies in his first play, *Jupiter*, see Thomas Moore, *Memoirs of the Life of the Right Honourable Richard Brinsley Sheridan* (London, 1825), p. 18; his later play *The Critic* contains a ridiculous internal play in 'true sentimental' style, 'and', goes on the ridiculous Mr Sneer, 'nothing ridiculous in it from the beginning to the end', see the New Mermaid edition, ed. David Crane (London, 1989), p. 13.

performance because of its sentimental characters: 'the exquisite refinement in [Faulkland's] disposition, opposed to the noble simplicity, tenderness, and candour of Julia's, gives rise to some of the most affecting sentimental scenes I ever remember to have met with'.[5] It was Sheridan's habit to criticise ideas by promoting them in a preposterous manner; he used this trick very successfully in his political career. Is the play's mawkish sentimentality itself an attack on sentimentality? Some have concluded that Sheridan coldly exploited the sentimental tastes of his audience in the Faulkland-Julia story, while raising questions about what he was doing in the parallel, unsentimental, tale of Lydia and Jack.[6]

What Sheridan's intentions were is hard to define because *The Rivals* maintains two untenable points of view at the same time. So, while Lydia is satirised for her *penchant* for sentimental novels, Faulkland's language is just such as those novels contain: 'I fear for her spirits, her health – her life! . . . If it rains, some shower may even then have chilled her delicate frame! If the wind be keen, some rude blast may have affected her! The heat of noon, the dews of the evening, may endanger the life of her for whom only I value mine' (II.i.95–103). The actress playing Julia, Mrs Bulkely, was given the important tenth night prologue in which sentimentalism is attacked, but also the sentimental last speech in *The Rivals*, which states that passion is dangerous and that virtue alone should be rewarded (a conclusion that does not sit happily with the rest of the play).[7] So did Sheridan have a genuine proclivity for sentimentality? Features of *The Rivals* – its aim at reforming the bad, its sympathy for the distressed – are copybook sentimentalism; and it was Sheridan's wife who had to be employed to excise some of the over-romanticised passages from the play, as marginal revisions show.[8] Perhaps Sheridan, a man of continually mixed emotions, actually had a Lydia-like yearning for sentimentality, for all his protestations to the contrary.

[5] *The Morning Chronicle*, 27 January 1775, quoted in John Loftis, *Sheridan and the Drama of Georgian England* (Oxford, 1976), p. 51.

[6] Mark S. Auburn, *Sheridan's Comedies* (Lincoln and London, 1977), p. 5; and Leonard J. Leff, 'Sheridan and Sentimentalism' in *Sheridan: Comedies Casebook* ed. Peter Davison (London, 1986), p. 59.

[7] As this prologue was probably only spoken on the tenth night itself, its attitudes may also be impermanent features of the play. See Tiffany Stern, *Rehearsal from Shakespeare to Sheridan* (Oxford, 2000), pp. 282–3, 288.

[8] Loftis, p. 10. For the idea that it was traditional to have a comic plot and a sentimental plot in sentimental plays, see Ernest Bernbaum, *The Drama of Sensibility* (Boston and London, 1915), p. 253. For the marginal revisions, see Walter Sichel, *Sheridan*, 2 vols (London, 1909), I, 469.

STRUCTURE

The Rivals begins where other plays end.[9] Lydia and Jack have met, fallen in love, and successfully courted each other before the play starts, as have Julia and Faulkland; in either case money is not a problem. Little actually happens during the course of the play: no one is, in fact, opposed to either of the nuptials, and no duel is ever fought. Faulkland's jealousy does not, ultimately, prevent his marriage to Julia; Lydia's sentimentalism does not get in the way of her marriage to Jack. Until the end of the play Bob Acres does not even talk to Lydia, and Mrs Malaprop does not meet her 'lover' Sir Lucius.[10] In the last scene, as soon as the mistaken identities are explained, both Sir Lucius and Acres drop their pretensions to Lydia with, seemingly, little heartache, before the whole group go off for a celebratory party. Every obstacle the play confronts is thus internal rather than external, arising from the emotions of the characters – the irascibility of Sir Anthony, the romanticism of Lydia and Faulkland, Acres' cowardice, Mrs Malaprop's linguistic pride.[11] The play has, for this reason, been compared to a Renaissance comedy of 'humours' in which the moods of the protagonists are the essence of the story.[12] Yet the characters in *The Rivals* do not develop and evolve as characters in 'humours' plays do: rather, they casually change their minds at the end of the play so that a happy ending is brought about – in the manner of a stock farce.[13] What can be the structure of a play in which so little happens?

The Rivals is shaped to personality and by the theatre – rather than structured by its narrative. Characters are paired, each being regularly confronted with their opposite: earthy, realistic Jack is linked with book-led Lydia; Mrs Malaprop's verbal confusion is matched by Sir Anthony's precision; Sir Lucius, a bold, antagonistic fighter, is pitted against Bob Acres, a coward; Julia's relaxed good humour is compared to the wilful melancholy of Faulkland.[14] Each excess is thus subtly parodied by being shown

---

[9] A point made by Fintan O'Toole, *A Traitor's Kiss: The Life of Richard Brinsley Sheridan* (London, 1997), p. 86.

[10] Pointed out by O'Toole, p. 86, and Moore, p. 104.

[11] A point made in Auburn, *Sheridan's Comedies*, p. 34.

[12] Louis Kronenberger, *The Thread of Laughter* (New York, 1952), p. 193. For the suggestion that the humour-like dispositions of the characters cripple character development, see Jack D. Durant, *Richard Brinsley Sheridan* (Boston, 1975), p. 75.

[13] For more on this, see Alan Rodway, 'Goldsmith and Sheridan: Satirists of Sentiment' in *Renaissance and Modern Essays* ed. G. R. Hibbard (London, 1966), p. 70.

[14] See Loftis, p. 51.

The earliest depiction of a performance of *The Rivals*, this engraving of IV.ii is from a variant title page for the 1776 edition of the play, described as being 'a Comedy as it is perform'd at the Theatre Royal in Covent Garden'. Bodleian Library, Shuttleworth 157.

in proximity to its opposite. And, whenever any character overreaches him- or herself, another character points it out – 'you are a truly moderate and polite arguer', says Sir Anthony to Mrs Malaprop, 'for almost every third word you say is on my side of the question' (I.ii.253–5).[15]

The Rivals, built out of opposites, features several individuals who take on alternative names and are thus, in themselves, contradictory. Mrs Malaprop pretends to be the young lover 'Delia' in her letters to Sir Lucius; Bob Acres bolsters his courage by inventing a brave fictional self, 'Fighting Bob'; Jack Absolute is the poverty-stricken 'Ensign Beverley' and the anonymous 'Mr Saunderson'. Partly this is the stuff of farce; partly it relates to larger themes: in *The Rivals* most characters are playing at being someone else. Lydia is pretending to be a romantic heroine, Acres to be a town fop, Lucy to be a simpleton. Faulkland makes out that he has killed a man in a duel when he has not; Lydia professes 'Beverley' has been unfaithful when he has not. So the play examines the contradictory nature of people, a theme that continually fascinated Sheridan. Of course, the characters in *The Rivals* learn to reject play-acting in favour of greater self-knowledge over the five acts. But the play really relishes irreconcilable opposites: Acres' habit of swearing with paired but opposing nouns ('whips and wheels') draws repeated attention to this, as does Lucy's interjection 'O gemini', referring to the twin stars Castor and Pollux (of which one is bright and one dim).

Theatrically the text is carefully designed. Its narrative gives omniscient knowledge to the audience who never have to share the characters' emotional worries, and can see the happy ending from the outset. The first scene summarises the story so far, whilst also providing social detail (Fag has been made pretentious by exposure to Bath; Thomas still has a country wholesomeness). In the last scene, as was characteristic of plays of the time, all the stage characters line up while one (in this instance, Julia), steps forward to give a moral to the story.[16] Internally, the play breaks comfortably into two halves, the misunderstandings being created in acts I-III, and resolved in acts IV-V. As spectators of the time could buy half-price tickets for entrance into the theatre after the first three acts were over, entertainments would often have a final two acts that were to some extent freestanding.[17] So it is with *The Rivals*: Sheridan had a profound understanding of contemporary theatre though he denied it (see his Preface, 68–82).

---

[15] See Robert Hogan, 'Plot, Character, and Comic Language in Sheridan' in *Comedy from Shakespeare to Sheridan* ed. A. R. Braunmuller and J. C. Bulman (Newark, 1986), p. 277.

[16] See C. B. Hogan, *The London Stage, Part V* (Carbondale, Illinois, 1968), lxxxix.

[17] Mark S. Auburn, 'Theatre in the age of Garrick and Sheridan' in *Sheridan Studies* ed. James Morwood and David Crane (Cambridge, 1995), p. 15.

THEMES

Why was this play of contradictions set in Bath? Partly because Bath was home of inconsistencies: a holiday resort constricted by regulations (see I.i.71–2 and note); a genteel town filled with social climbers trying to acquire 'polish', as Acres's conversations with David and Fag's advice to Thomas illustrate. Writers relished Bath's paradoxes: in Bath 'even the wives and daughters of low tradesmen . . . hobble country-dances and cotillions among lordlings, 'squires, counsellors, and clergy', observed Tobias Smollett; Jane Austen commented that Bath was cheaper than London and one might there 'be important at comparatively little expense', a notion that appealed to impoverished aristocrats like Sir Lucius and, perhaps, Sir Anthony.[18] To Bath spa came the gouty and ill seeking relief from their aches by drinking or bathing in the foul-smelling hot waters; with them came the young and healthy, seeking romance. Together young and old, fit and infirm, gathered and, as one contemporary poem had it, boiled like a stew.[19] Clearly *The Rivals* is, on one level, one of many social comedies not only set in, but about, the way society is shaped by and to Bath.

The play has a number of social themes. For instance, the epilogue to *The Rivals* advises women to have the 'sense and merit' to shame men into acquiring knowledge (52–7). This is the very same proposal Sheridan had put forward in 1774, a year before writing *The Rivals*, in a serious manifesto called *The Royal Sanctuary*. The idea behind *The Royal Sanctuary* was that a place should be established where well-born women could go to be educated: men were more likely to strive intellectually and morally, believed Sheridan, if women set high standards for them to live up to. But despite advocating that women should be taught the arts, music, sewing, riding, domestic science and history, Sheridan stressed that women in the sanctuary should avoid novels. Books of that kind, he wrote, show 'human nature depraved' and might corrupt the reader.[20] So it is with *The Rivals*, where Sheridan's message seems to be that women *should* be literate and *should* read – but only certain books. Lydia and Mrs Malaprop both show different versions of misreading (the one reading the 'wrong' books, the other gleaning the wrong information from them). Yet, as the play also

[18] Tobias Smollett, *The Expedition of Humphry Clinker* (1771) quoted here from Peter Miles's Everyman edition of that book (London, 1993), p. 39; Jane Austen, *Persuasion* (1818), quoted here from the Penguin Classic ed. Gillian Beer (London, 1998), p. 15.

[19] *Bath: its Beauties, and Amusements*, (second edition, 1777), p. 3: 'Where free from ling'ring Education's plan, / By which the Brute is polish'd into Man, / We learn a shorter and more pleasing road, / And grow (like beef) by stewing—Alamode'.

[20] Quoted in Durant, p. 77.

maintains, the men are partly responsible for the women's waywardness. Jack has humoured Lydia's romance instead of stamping it out (IV.ii.192–4), Sir Anthony wishes to keep women illiterate instead of directing their learning (I.ii.214–7). The play, like *The Royal Sanctuary*, promotes the education of women, but for – and regulated by – men.

The Rivals also considers women's natures. It presents a world in which a cunning woman like Lucy finds it better to be thought 'simple' than to show wit; in which a woman who has tried – albeit unsuccessfully – to acquire sophisticated vocabulary is a figure of fun; in which woman's sexuality is often ridiculous or repulsive: Faulkland most dreads being 'linked . . . to some antique virago, whose gnawing passions and long-hoarded spleen shall make me curse my folly half the day and all the night!' (III.ii.122–4). So is this a feminist play or the reverse? The answer is double-edged. Julia, with her unaffected learning, her faithfulness, her modesty, her forgiving nature seems to be the play's model woman. Theatre tricks are employed to secure regular applause for Julia: while Lydia opens her scene already on stage, Julia enters mid-scene, ensuring a burst of approbation for her first appearance; the actress playing Julia was given the important tenth night prologue and the greatly admired epilogue. The point seems to be that, unlike the other women, 'amiable and elegant Julia' has profited from being allowed to be her 'own mistress' (I.ii.107).[21] Sheridan, then, may have intended to show that educated women, given a limited freedom, will naturally reveal maturity and good sense. Yet he undercuts this purpose by his portrayal: Julia is the least compelling character in the play.

Eighteenth-century hypocrisy in its various forms is continually – but gently – harped on in *The Rivals*. In particular the play examines the contrast between refined language and the unrefined preoccupations it masks. Most of the characters in the play are more clearly concerned with money than, as they claim, with love. Jack could, he tells Faulkland, have married Lydia long ago, but he is holding out because he wants her fortune; Sir Lucius, who is penniless, also yearns for Lydia's money; Lucy sells letters and secrets for clothes and coins; Sir Anthony promises Jack a fortune – if he marries it. Even Lydia is obsessed with money: she wishes, specifically, to marry someone who is not rich, and to forfeit her fortune into the bargain. Searching for a metaphor, Fag compares lying to a forged cheque, while Faulkland decides that if Julia is true metal he will be prepared to coin her and stamp his name on the product. Only Julia is content to give up wealth – in the knowledge of what she is renouncing (V.i.43–6): Julia alone values affection aside from capital.

---

[21] Sheridan in *The Morning Chronicle* 29 January–1 February 1775, quoted in Leff, p. 63.

Yet for all its gesturing towards serious issues, *The Rivals* has a surreal quality that takes the edge off it as social satire. Much like *The Importance of Being Earnest*, it takes place in an upside-down world that looks a little like ours – but from a different perspective.[22] The topsy-turvy world of *The Rivals* allowed Sheridan to be critical while being frivolous; by turning convention onto its head, he could show it to be essentially ridiculous (the absurd things Mrs Malaprop believes 'do not become a young woman' are amusing partly because they are a criticism of laughable rules that defined woman's behaviour).

In the back-to-front world of *The Rivals*, language and meaning are not entirely linked and vocabulary in the play is often slippery. 'Unripe judgment' wrote Thomas Sheridan, Richard's father, is all too often 'perverted from sense to sound'; *The Rivals* seems to comment on a lack of clarity as a characteristic of eighteenth-century society.[23] Acres uses words that sound as though they might be French, 'squallante, rumblante, and quiverante' (II.i.199), but are in fact his creation. Mrs Malaprop does not make up new words, but applies words of one meaning to a place where one sounding similar is required. Even characters who do not misuse words still continually abuse language. 'A circulating library in a town is as an evergreen tree of diabolical knowledge!' says Sir Anthony, 'they who are so fond of handling the leaves will long for the fruit at last' (I.ii.225–8), sliding from 'leaves' as book-pages to 'leaves' on trees. Books, the repository of language, are the main props in *The Rivals* and they are thrust into one another, employed for pressing lace or torn to make curl papers.[24] Against this, a desperate attempt is made to force language to be logical – Acres will not use the usual imprecise swearwords but invents new, situationally relevant, oaths. Precision and randomness vary extraordinarily; in eighteenth-century Bath, suggests the play, it was hard to differentiate sense from nonsense.

CHARACTERS: WOMEN

Would we think of Lydia as 'languishing' if it were not for her name? True, the lady is first presented on a sofa, but her mind is filled with excitement not

---

[22] O'Toole, pp. 93–4.

[23] Thomas Sheridan, *A Plan of Education for the Young Nobility and Gentry of Great Britain* (1769), p. 101.

[24] Christine S. Wiesenthal observes that 'When Lydia not very languidly jams *The Innocent Adultery* between the chaste covers of *The Whole Duty of Man* ... she imparts an entirely new dimension of physicality to the notion of literary subtexts' in 'Representation and Experimentation in the Major Comedies of Richard Brinsley Sheridan', *Eighteenth Century Studies* 25 (1992) pp. 309–330 (314).

Mrs Malaprop (Margaret Rutherford), Jack Absolute (Robin Ellis), and Lydia Languish (Marilyn Taylerson), III.iii, in the 1966 Theatre Royal Haymarket production of the *The Rivals*. Photograph by Angus McBean.

offered by her life, her nature is stubborn, her body disturbingly alluring. What is happening through the play – in which Lydia moves from sofa, to chair, to Kingsmead Fields – is that Lydia is becoming, in advance of marrying Jack, increasingly energetic and increasingly 'absolute'. From the first there was nothing yielding about Lydia; for all her bookish romanticism, she showed little sympathy for her aunt's romantic yearnings, and scant regard for Julia's affections.[25] And far from being, as Mrs Malaprop and Sir Anthony believe, a victim of soppy reading, Lydia actually forces a novelistic romanticism onto other characters: Acres, Sir Lucius, and Jack, as himself and as Beverley, all agree to fight duels for her love. Lydia, who begins the play with mesmerising eyes through which she, metaphorically, squints ('She squints, don't she?' (III.i.51), 'When her *love-eye* was fixed on *me*, t' other, her *eye* of *duty*, was finely obliqued' (IV.iii.75–7)), finally learns to see properly. Confronting her true feelings, it is she who, at the end of *The Rivals*, boldly proposes to Jack (V.iii.194–6): she is, indeed, Absolute already.

Lydia shares with Mrs Malaprop the habit of speaking a language formed from books. The family resemblance does not go further than that, however: each woman makes different mistakes, and each has a different surname – Lydia is not Malaprop. It is Mrs Malaprop who provokes much of the play's laughter, and that is for the single, continually repeated joke of verbal misapplication, a humour that the actor-manager David Garrick had feared 'very nearly Exhausted' even in 1766.[26] But Mrs Malaprop reinvigorated the comedy of misusing words partly because so much of what she says 'wrong' is also 'right'.[27] When Mrs Malaprop compliments Jack on the 'ingenuity' of his appearance she reminds the audience that he is ingeniously pretending to be two people at the same time (III.iii.2); when she says she has 'proof controvertible' (I.ii.192) of Lydia's wayward affections, she illustrates that her proof is indeed 'controvertible' (debatable). 'In unerringly choosing the wrong word', writes Christopher Ricks, 'she is a great one for getting on a right relation. She is mistress of the household misappliances.'[28] Mrs Malaprop even abuses the language of language – 'conjunctions' instead of 'injunctions', 'preposition' meaning 'proposition', 'allegory' for 'alligator' – in her misuse of linguistic terms

[25] Katharine Worth, *Sheridan and Goldsmith* (London, 1992), p. 130.

[26] Auburn, *Sheridan's Comedies*, p. 38. The joke has been of importance to linguists and philosophers, however, as it shows 'meaning' can be conveyed independently of words. See Donald Davidson's famous 'A Nice Derangement of Epitaphs', in *Truth and Interpretation: Perspectives on the Philosophy of Donald Davidson*, ed. Ernest LePore, (Oxford, 1986), pp. 433–446.

[27] See Durant, p. 70; Worth, p. 129; Elizabeth Duthie, *The Rivals* (London, 1979), xxvi.

[28] Christopher Ricks, 'Word Making and Mistaking' in *The State of the Language* ed. Christopher Ricks and Leonard Michaels (London, 1990), p. 464; Richard Sheridan, *The School for Scandal and Other Plays*, ed. Michael Cordner (Oxford, 1998), xi.

she becomes a footnote to the source of her own error. Indeed, the variety of mistake she makes show that this 'queen of the dictionary' (II.ii.37–8) has, indeed, been reading dictionaries and books of grammar. As Sheridan's father wrote dictionaries and grammars, Mrs Malaprop may be an attack on everything Thomas Sheridan stood for: Malaprop's characterisation, suggests Fintan O'Toole, 'is a hint that too much concern with the niceties of language can derange the mind'.[29]

At the end of the play, Mrs Malaprop is forced, cruelly, to take stock in a way that does not involve malapropisms – for all that the character is a forerunner of the pantomime dame, the single moment of tragedy in the play is hers. After the humiliation of being refused by Sir Lucius and Acres – just when everyone else is making marriage plans – Mrs Malaprop leaves Kingsmead Fields. Her final line, 'Men are all barbarians!' (V.iii.239), is free of the malapropisms that up until now have defined the character. What Mrs Malaprop says is 'meant' – and is not ridiculous. Interestingly, in the original, kinder, version of the play (see Appendix), Mrs Malaprop ended the play contracted to Sir Lucius: it is telling that this saccharine conclusion was damned by the first audience and the darker ending has come to be preferred.

CHARACTERS: MEN

It is a feature of the back-to-front world of *The Rivals* that Sir Anthony should have been played by Edward ('Ned') Shuter (c. 1728–1776), a man of about forty-five, while his handsome son Jack was played by Henry Woodward (1714–1777), a man of sixty-one. The boundaries between old and young are confused in *Rivals*; those who have to submit to the rules are more sensible than those who make them. Nor was it that Woodward was habitually cast as a young hero, for a part he had recently played was in Samuel Foote's *The Maid of Bath* (performed at the Haymarket, London, in 1771), which told the true story of Elizabeth Linley, later to become Sheridan's wife. In *The Maid* Woodward played lust-driven but wheelchair-bound Sir Christopher Cripple; Sheridan, knowing the audience partly expected his *Rivals* to provide the next instalment of *The Maid*, seems to have flouted expectations on every count.

Jack Absolute shares with his father a name that is a quality: both are 'absolute' meaning inflexible and in this way both are perfect matches for the strong women. Neither is entirely likeable. Jack is the nearest character to a Restoration rake, calculating with his love and exploitative with his friendship. He could have brought Lydia to marriage long ago, he tells Faulkland,

[29] O'Toole, p. 88.

but is holding back in order to secure her fortune (II.i.64–6); he fools his father and tricks his friends, ensuring that Faulkland is upset by Acres and that Acres feels forced, against his will, to challenge 'Beverley'. Yet we do not dislike Jack, largely because of the way the character is theatricalised. The part is filled with asides to ensure that the audience see things from Jack's perspective: when Acres is told he made Faulkland 'a little jealous' (II.i.275), the understatement, which Bob will not appreciate, is for us.[30]

Jack is a symbol of the internal contradictions in the play. 'Who the devil are you?' (IV.ii.106–7) asks Sir Anthony, but the question redounds throughout the text. According to himself Jack is both 'Ensign Beverley' and 'Captain Jack Absolute'; when he meets his father unexpectedly he is 'Mr Saunderson'. Playing many roles, the character is also frequently denied his actual name. The furious Sir Anthony will not say 'Jack' until his son will accept an unknown bride; he opts instead for 'dog' and 'puppy' – until the insult '"jack"-anapes' escapes his lips (II.i.418); when Lydia is angry with her lover she, too, eschews 'Jack', giving him instead a cold 'Sir' (IV.ii.169). When Jack confesses who he really is, all the other characters drop their pretences and reveal their true selves as well: Jack thus seems in control of the action. Indeed, some critics have regarded the many-faceted Jack as an 'Everyman'; he is, after all, conscious of the foibles of every character.[31] But he is too idiosyncratic to be thought of as an objective observer. In a play in which names are more than names, it is significant that Jack is so often deprived of his sobriquet; significant, too, that he is never known by his full name of 'John' (V.i.161). He, like other characters, tries to win love by being someone else; he, too, has to learn to be liked as himself.

Sir Anthony appears to show what Jack will become. Both are Absolute, both romantic (Sir Anthony eloped with Jack's mother), both are highly conscious of the charms of Lydia. But does the irascible Sir Anthony offer hope for the future of young Jack (he is, behind everything, a loving father)? Or does he show that lack of self-knowledge and understanding will be perpetuated over time?

The patronising Faulkland, replete with French valet, Du Peigne, is a snob. He is also petulant, and incapable of trusting the woman who adores him. He cruelly exploits the fact that he is to be a harmless second in Jack's duel, pretending to his distraught fiancée that he himself has fought a duel and killed a man. Yet Sheridan loved the character. In a Drury Lane prompt-script for a 1790s revival of The Rivals, Julia's explanation of Faulkland's nature (I.ii.113–32), cut by the actors, is angrily annotated in Sheridan's hand: 'The only Speech in

---

[30] A point made by Worth, pp. 44, 117.
[31] Auburn, Sheridan's Comedies, p. 50.

Sir Anthony Absolute (Michael Hordern) eats his egg, III.i, in the National Theatre 1983/84 production. Photograph by Zoe Dominic.

the Play that cannot be omitted. The Pruning Knife! Damme, the Axe, the Hatchet!'[32] Sheridan, then, particularly regarded the moment when Faulkland's caprice is excused; he continually maintained that the character would 'improve on the audience the more it is understood'.[33] But what is there to understand? Contemporaries traced this protective attitude to the fact that Faulkland *was* Sheridan. 'When I became acquainted with Sheridan,' wrote his son's tutor, 'I was at no loss to discern where he had found the character of Faulkland'.[34] Perhaps that explains why Faulkland's faults are better depicted than resolved.

Acres shows to what extent Sheridan used the characteristics of his actors in his writing. Bob leaves his dog, his horse, his mother, to go to Bath and learn sophistication, changing his dress, taking dance lessons, growing his hair. He is part of the play's visual humour, and, as is continually pointed out, he looks ludicrous. The actor John Quick (1748–1831), who performed Acres, was famous for his amusing appearance – for he was 'tiny', a 'blithe dwarf'.[35] Acres' small stature will have provided an additional, long awaited, joke at the end of the play: when finally confronted, Lydia will have towered over her inamorato. Acres is the clown of the play, and statements like 'I'll make myself small enough' (V.iii.44–5), take on a new meaning in the light of the performer who spoke them.

Fag and David mirror their masters. Fag is proud of his Bath airs, scheming, cares little for truth, but is loyal to friends. David is simple, devoted, an unreformed rustic who sees no value in pretension. Interestingly, the actor who played David, John Dunstall (1717–1778), actually had some of the mannerisms that may have inspired Sheridan's creation of Mrs Malaprop. He 'was remarkable for his affectation of Grecisms, and words of many syllables – insomuch, that when he was missing at a Rehearsal, Ned Shuter told the . . . Manager, that Dunstall had found out another hard word, and was gone to Whitechapel with it'.[36] For his characters, then, Sheridan used a mixture of the theatre and his life, just as he did with the themes of his play.

---

[32] Crompton Rhodes, *Harlequin Sheridan* (Oxford, 1933), p. 144.

[33] *The Morning Chronicle*, 29 January–1 February 1775, quoted in Leff, p. 63.

[34] R. L. Purdy, *The Rivals, A Comedy, edited from the Larpent MS* (Oxford, 1935), xliv. See also Elizabeth Inchbald, 'Remarks' in *Sheridan: Comedies Casebook* ed. Davison, p. 84: 'It is supposed, by the author's most intimate friends, that, in delineating Faulkland, he took a discerning view of his own disposition, in all the anxious tenderness of a youthful lover'; James Boaden, *Memoirs of Mrs Siddons*, 2 vols (1827), I, 249: 'Falkland expresses . . . the captious alarms of the author's own passion for Miss Linley'.

[35] Anthony Pasquin, pseud. (actually John Williams), *The Children of Thespis. A Poem, part the third, the second edition* (1786–88), p. 51–2.

[36] Anthony Pasquin, pseud. (actually John Williams), *The Pin-Basket to the Children of Thespis* (1797), p. 142.

DATE AND HISTORICAL CONTEXT

The Rivals was 'a decided attempt to . . . follow up the blow [to sentimental-ism] which Goldsmith had given', and Goldsmith's *She Stoops to Conquer* was pointedly performed four days before the opening night of *Rivals*.[37] Five actors appeared in both plays and their parts are closely related: Mrs Jane Green, who played social-climbing older women, was Mrs Hardcastle and Mrs Malaprop; Mrs Mary Bulkley, who played lively young beauties, was Kate Hardcastle and Julia; Ned Shuter, who played cantankerous old gentlemen, was Mr Hardcastle and Sir Anthony; John Quick, who played unremittingly country types, was Tony Lumpkin and Bob Acres; arrogant Lee Lewes was Young Marlowe and Faulkland. Newspapers immediately picked up on the comparison: *The Public Ledger* called Acres a 'second Tony Lumpkin'.[38] *The Rivals*, first performed on 17 January 1775, was the only new comic mainpiece mounted at Covent Garden in the 1774–5 season; it was to be a new star play in the mode of *She Stoops*.

Samuel Johnson later called *The Rivals* one of the 'two best comedies of the age' (the other being Sheridan's comic opera *The Duenna*).[39] But the play flopped on its first night. This will have been a surprise to its author who had told his father-in-law some days before performance '[Covent Garden's manager] . . . and some of his friends . . . assure me in the most flattering terms that there is not a doubt of [*The Rivals*'] success'; it will have shocked the actor David Garrick, who had heard there was 'great Expectation in ye Publick' about the production, and it will have mortified the actors who had already put it about that the play was 'the *ne plus ultra* of Comedy'.[40] But from the first not much pleased the audience about *The Rivals* – except for the epilogue, said by some to have been written by Sheridan's wife, by oth-ers to have been written by Garrick.[41] The comedy was 'so intolerably long, and so decidedly opposed in its composition to the taste of the day, as to draw down a degree of censure', wrote an actor who was present on the open-ing night; one newspaper of the time described the audience leaving the theatre asking 'Well, sir, have not you been vastly fatigued tonight?'[42] Other problems with the text were its crude passages and its excessive malapropisms: 'the plot was not happily chosen, nor skilfully conducted, the characters had

[37] John Bernard, *Retrospections of the Stage*, 2 vols (London, 1830), I, 142.

[38] Edition of 18 January 1775, quoted in Richard C. Taylor, '"Future Retrospection": Reread-ing Sheridan's Reviewers' in *Sheridan Studies* ed. James Morwood and David Crane (Cambridge, 1995), p. 49.

[39] Quoted in Stanley Ayling, *A Portrait of Sheridan* (London, 1985), p. 47.

[40] Richard Brinsley Sheridan, *The Letters*, ed. Cecil Price, 3 vols (Oxford, 1966), I, 85; quoted in James Morwood, *The Life and Works of Richard Brinsley Sheridan* (Edinburgh, 1985), p. 34; *The Morning Chronicle*, 19 January 1775 quoted Purdy, xviii.

[41] For the epilogue, see O'Toole, p. 86 and Sichel, I, 498.

[42] Bernard, I, 142; John Hampden, *An Eighteenth-Century Journal* (London, 1940), p. 134.

no great claim to novelty, and . . . puns, witticism, similes and metaphors [were no] substitutes for polished diction'.[43] Most serious was the accusation that the play was prejudiced in its depiction of the Irish.

The fault for the first night fiasco did not entirely lie with Sheridan. Ned Shuter (Sir Anthony) 'did not know any two lines together, and wherever he was out, he tried to fill the interval with oaths and buffoonery'.[44] John Lee (Sir Lucius), fluffed his lines, while his Irish accent was 'a horrid mixture of discordant brogues', 'an uncouth dialect, neither Welch, English nor Irish': the only time he mastered the pronunciation was when an apple was thrown at him 'and with a genuine rich brogue, [he] angrily cried out, "by the pow'rs, is it *personal*? – is it me, or the matter?"'[45] In addition, organised groups ('claques') had been mustered amongst the audience to do down the play. Some were friends of Mathews, the man with whom Sheridan had recently fought a couple of duels (see 'Author' below); some were friends of Mathews's second, the Irishman William Barnett, who suspected Sir Lucius was written as an attack on him.[46] Spectators did indeed find the play full of Irish prejudice, their opinions probably shaped by Barnett. 'A Briton' in *The Morning Post* declared: 'it is the first time I ever remember to have seen so villainous a portrait of an Irish Gentleman permitted so openly to insult that country upon the boards of an English theatre'.[47] In addition, a separate claque seems to have been formed in support of an author whose play had been rejected in favour of Sheridan's (see Preface, 88–96). With predetermined enemies and an overlong and badly acted first performance, *The Rivals* was doomed; it was withdrawn from the stage 'to undergo some severe prunings, trimmings, and patchings, before its second performance'.[48] It is a version of the text used from the second performance onwards that is provided here and in most editions.[49]

In revision Sheridan seriously altered his text. Malapropisms were removed from other characters and confined to Mrs Malaprop; crude jokes were taken out of the production altogether. No longer does Sir Anthony propose that Jack marry a lady he has never seen with the suggestive 'there

---

[43] Purdy, xv.

[44] *The Morning Post*, 30 January 1775, quoted in Purdy, xvi.

[45] The first is from *The Morning Chronicle* 20 January 1775, the second from *The Morning Chronicle*, 18 January 1775 both quoted in Purdy, xvii; the third is from Frederick Reynolds, *The Life and Times of Frederick Reynolds*, 2 vols in 1 (London, 1826,) II, 228.

[46] Purdy, xii.

[47] *The Morning Post*, 21 January 1775, quoted in Loftis, p. 54.

[48] *The Morning Post*, 19 January 1775, quoted in Purdy, xx.

[49] Though advanced publicity had already advertised that *The Rivals* would be performed on 29 November, almost certainly a second night performance of the condemned text did not in fact take place.

are many things, you have never seen, which I believe, you would have no aversion to'; nor does he later accuse Jack of being the kind of 'lifeless . . . clod' who would lie with Lydia 'like a cucumber, on a hot bed'; or, on finding Jack's 'trinket' to be a sword, say 'get along . . . and let her know you have better trinkets than that'.[50] Sir Lucius does not expostulate that Lady Dorothy Wriggle was stolen from him by a 'little son of a whore of a Major' (but that Lady Dorothy Carmine was taken by a 'little rogue of a major' IV.iii.4–5). The plot is altered too: Sir Lucius is no longer just a fortune-hunter, content to marry Mrs Malaprop when he finds out who he has been wooing (see Appendix). For the amended version of *The Rivals*, the part of Sir Lucius was recast and given to Lawrence Clinch (d. 1812), an actual Irishman. The new, nobler, genuinely Irish Sir Lucius, proposes to fight a duel specifically to defend his nation against insult. David Garrick, manager of the rival theatre, watched the revised *Rivals* played eleven days after its unsuccessful first performance, on 28 January 1775, and remarked early in the evening, 'I see this play will creep'. At the end he had to say 'I see this play will run'.[51]

The change of direction *The Rivals* had undergone affected every aspect of production right up to the choice of afterpiece. The condemned first performance had been followed by *The Chaplet*, a musical entertainment about 'Damon' who leaves the faithful Laura to flirt with jilted Pastora. Though Damon is finally forced to take his first lover back, the union is grudging and the afterpiece is frankly unromantic.[52] The revised play in its opening performance was flanked by *Thomas and Sally*, a musical entertainment about the faithful Sally who awaits the equally faithful Tom who has gone to sea. A passing squire threatens her virtue, but just in time her lover returns. The end of the play promotes marriage, love, and loyalty to one's partner and country. Says Tom:

> . . . while mighty George has foes,
> On land, and main, their malice I'll oppose.
> But hang this talking, my desires are keen;
> You see yon steeple, and know what I mean.[53]

The new *Rivals* upheld British values freed from moral ambiguity. Everything, including the choice of afterpieces, was designed to illustrate this.

---

[50] Purdy, pp. 33, 47, 104.
[51] Quoted in Richard Sheridan, *The Rivals*, ed. Cecil Price (Oxford, 1968), p. 10.
[52] Moses Mendez, *The Chaplet: a Musical Entertainment in Verse* (1749), p. 4.
[53] Isaac Bickerstaff, *Thomas and Sally: or, the Sailor's Return* (1765), p. 20.

Recent Stage History

Sheridan told Lady Cork that *The Rivals* 'was one of the worst plays in the language, and he would give anything he had not written it'.[54] He harboured, throughout his life, a desire to rework the play again – though he seems never to have done so.[55] Yet the play has been consistently popular both on page and on stage. Dickens paid *The Rivals* homage in his depiction of Squeers – described in *Nicholas Nickleby* as having 'but one eye' when 'the popular prejudice runs in favour of two' (see *Rivals*, III.i.89–90); these days the linguistic agility of George Bush and Dan Quayle ensure that Mrs Malaprop's name is seldom off newspaper front pages.[56] Moreover, the play has, from its inception, been in regular performance in Europe and America. It was first played in the USA in the John Street Theatre, New York, in 1778; at the same time it was also put on by the young Kotzebue in Germany (extraordinarily, with the parts of Julia and Acres doubled).[57] Its continuing fame probably relates to the very fact that it is not entirely 'complete' – it is malleable and, like a pantomime, readily accepts ad libs and additions. Prompt books recording the Malaprop of the Louisa Lane Drew (in Joseph Jefferson's production of *Rivals*, Arch Street Theatre, Philadelphia, 1879) give 266 alterations to the role including the observation that Jack is 'graceful as a young gazette' and Beverley a 'conceited young pendant'; Jefferson himself, famous for his depiction of Bob Acres, made 'sweeping alterations' to the whole play.[58] In the National Theatre's famous *Rivals* of 1983 Geraldine McEwan's poignantly brittle Mrs Malaprop marched off the stage proclaiming 'Men are all Bavarians'.[59]

The parts that are always a problem for directors are Julia and Faulkland, who, by the turn of the nineteenth century, were frequently revised out of productions altogether.[60] Peter Wood's National Theatre *Rivals* handled the characters superbly, with Fiona Shaw playing a Julia whose yearning emotion was continually frustrated by Faulkland, performed by the talented

---

[54] Purdy, lii.

[55] Purdy, li.

[56] Charles Dickens, *Nicholas Nickleby* (1838), chapter 4, quoted here from the Penguin Classic edition ed. Mark Ford (London, 1999), p. 44.

[57] Sichel, I, 497.

[58] Mark S. Auburn, 'The Pleasures of Sheridan's *The Rivals*: A Critical Study in the Light of Stage History', *Modern Philology*, 72 (1975), pp. 256–71 (265); Joseph Jefferson, *The Autobiography* ed. Alan S. Downer (Cambridge, Massachusetts, 1964), p. 297.

[59] See Robert Cushman's review of the National Theatre production of 1983 in *The Observer*, reprinted in *The London Theatre Record* for 9–22 April 1983, p. 269.

[60] See George Henry Nettleton, 'Mr Joseph Jefferson's Acting version of The Rivals' in *The Major Dramas of Sheridan* (Boston, 1906), pp. 323–5.

Bob Acres (Joseph Jefferson) and Sir Lucius O'Trigger (William Florence), V.i.
Photograph by B. J. Falk, 1891.

and underrated Edward Petherbridge. Petherbridge's Faulkland, his character as high pitched as his Edinburgh accent, was 'a self-destructive neurotic who typically smoothes out his beloved's drawing-paper after she has intemperately crunched it'.[61] The production included Michael Hordern's gouty Sir Anthony whose lusty relish for serving-maid and Lydia alike brought out the play's pervasive sexual undertone, and raised questions about what Jack would become. Particularly memorable was the scene where Sir Anthony determined never to forgive Jack while eating a boiled egg: he inverted the shell and smashed it rhythmically with his spoon to the words 'never, never, never', which brilliantly underlined his own 'absolute' childishness. Geraldine McEwan performed a Mrs Malaprop quivering with frightened superiority – every wrong word was carefully sought for and found with triumphant relief; a similar 'dotty hauteur' was adopted by Wendy Craig in the Royal Shakespeare Company's *Rivals* (2000).[62] These later, affecting Malaprops, are a new take on what has traditionally been played as an imperious character of the Lady-Bracknell type, tremendously performed by those great comic dames of twentieth-century theatre, Dame Margaret Rutherford (1966) and Dame Edith Evans (1941) and (1971).

The scenery that flanks *The Rivals* has always been important. *The Rivals* is about interiority and exteriority in people, and the interior and exterior of Bath houses are carefully differentiated in the text to mirror this. Even on the unsuccessful first night in 1775, 'Scorpion' in *The Morning Post* recorded that 'a perspective view through the south parade at Bath, to the late Mr. Allen's delightful villa, was universally admired'; for the first Bath performance later in 1775 Mary Linley wrote to her sister that 'There was a new scene of the N. Parade, painted by Mr. Davis, and a most delightful one . . . Every body says . . . that yours in town is not so good'.[63] Setting is an element of the play; as Nicholas de Jong observed of John Gunter's 1983 National Theatre designs (a revolving Bath façade with an 'interior' on its reverse): 'the play's true hero is Bath itself, a watering pace where the rich and modish washed their fine (and dirty) linen in public while playing with love and the marriage market'.[64]

---

[61] Michael Billington, review of the National Theatre 1983 production in *London Theatre Record*, p. 269.

[62] Benedict Nightingale, review of the 2000 Royal Shakespeare Company production in *The Times*, 3 April 2000, reprinted in *Theatre Record* for 25 March to 7 April 2000, p. 438.

[63] Purdy, xv; Moore, p. 103.

[64] *Mail on Sunday*, in *London Theatre Record*, p. 270.

NOTE ON THE TEXT

The Rivals was first printed in 1775, reissued the same year, and printed again with variations in 1776. The 1776 version appears to have been set from a copy of the 1775 text containing manuscript additions and cuts by Sheridan.[65] For this reason the edition of 1775 is used here as the copy-text, though variants from the 1776 edition are preferred. An earlier text of *The Rivals* survives in manuscript; it is the copy that was sent to the Lord Chamberlain for approval before performance and is thus similar to the version of the play performed, and damned, on the first night.[66] Two significant scenes from it are supplied in an appendix.

The prologue for the unsuccessful first night survives in Sheridan's hand in the Amelia Edwards collection at Somerville College, Oxford; it is printed by Cecil Price.[67] The prologue provided in the 1775 edition will have been spoken from the second (successful) performance until the ninth; it is printed here flanked by the prologue for the tenth night from the 1776 edition. A manuscript fragment of that tenth night prologue survives in Sheridan's hand in the British Library; variants from it are used to elucidate the printed prologue.[68] The preface, absent in the 1776 text, is provided here from the 1775 edition.

In the text that follows spelling and punctuation are modernised; 'pho' is rendered 'foh', 'phrenzy', 'frenzy', and 'huzzy', 'hussy'; 'devil', 'damn' and 'zounds' have been expanded (from 'd——l', 'd——n', 'z——ds' respectively). Italics have been preserved as they occur in some unlikely places and seem to indicate emphases – a subject of great interest to elocutionists like Sheridan, who is described watching his play *Pizarro* and repeating every syllable after each performer 'counting poetically the measure on his fingers'.[69] Dashes, however, which are used liberally but differently in surviving manuscripts and editions of the play, seem not to have a fixed meaning; they are not retained. Textual errors have been silently corrected in II.i.299 and III.iii.85. Songs and sections of books, originally in italics, are in quotation marks. Names have been regularised: 'Coachman' is Thomas, 'Captain Absolute' is

---

[65] See the notes to *The Dramatic Works of Richard Brinsley Sheridan*, ed. Cecil Price, 2 vols (Oxford, 1973), I, 58–66.

[66] Huntington Library, Larpent MS 383, transcribed and printed in full by Richard Little Purdy in *The Rivals, a Comedy: As it was First Acted at the Theatre-Royal in Covent-Garden* (Oxford, 1935).

[67] 'The First Prologue to The Rivals', *RES*, NS 20 (1969), pp. 192–5.

[68] Discussed in Robert A. H. Smith's 'Sheridan's Second Prologue to the Rivals: A Further Note', *Notes and Queries* N.S. 37 (1990), pp. 314–5.

[69] James Boaden, *The Life of Mrs. Jordan*, 2 vols (London, 1831), II, 16–17.

Jack Absolute. Stage-directions, which often occur mid-speech and are only sometimes bracketed, are provided here in round brackets and inserted before the speech they concern; all editorial stage-directions are in square brackets.

SOURCES

Numerous sources have been suggested for *The Rivals*. Lydia is close to the heroine of George Colman's *Polly Honeycombe* and to Biddy Tipkin in Richard Steele's *The Tender Husband*; Sir Anthony recalls Sir Sampson Legend from Congreve's *Love for Love*; Jack may relate to Atall in Colley Cibber's *The Double Gallant*; Bob Acres' 'sentimental swearing' seems to derive from Wittol in Congreve's *Old Bachelor*; the Julia-Faulkland plot may parody Arthur Murphy's *All in the Wrong*; while the main plot has elements in it that evoke Garrick's *Miss in her Teens* and Colman's *The Deuce is in Him*. The tracing of sources, however, is confused by the fact that Sheridan claimed to have none and to know little about the theatre: as his parents were playwright-actors, this is unlikely, but what Sheridan is keen to impress on readers in his preface is that he is doing something new – and is not a plagiarist.

In fact Sheridan was heavily reliant on the theatre of his time, as well as on his parents' writings, his own writings, and the story of his life: much of the content of *The Rivals* was 'borrowed' but so reshaped as to become Sheridan's own. His father's afterpiece *Captain O'Blunder* is probably the inspiration for the comic Irishman Sir Lucius; the name Faulkland may come from his mother's novel *Miss Sidney Biddulph*. His mother's play *A Journey to Bath*, rejected by Garrick in the 1760s, contains a prototype for Mrs Malaprop in the character of Mrs Tryfort. She is 'fondest of hard words, which without miscalling, she always takes care to misapply' (see *Rivals* I.ii.152–4), she talks of 'a progeny of learning' (see I.ii.233) and 'contagious countries' (see I.ii.245), and she insists that 'so much taciturnity doesn't become a young man' (see I.ii.186–7). In the same play is a character called Sir Jonathan Bull who anticipates Sir Lucius in his declaration 'if I had your ladyship at Bull Hall, I could show you a line of ancestry that would convince you we are not a people of yesterday . . . Why, the land and mansion house has slipped through our fingers, but, thank Heaven, the family pictures are still extant' (see III.iv.92–7).[70]

---

[70] See Rhodes, *Harlequin Sheridan*, p. 57, Durant, p. 69, Sichel, I, 492.

Mostly it was Sheridan's friends and family who supplied matter for *The Rivals*. Elizabeth Linley took the 'love name' that Mrs Malaprop adopts, 'Delia', during her courtship with Sheridan; 'elude her vigilance' (see III.iii.64–5) is a phrase from a letter by Elisabeth about the impossibility of outwitting her mother.[71] The song 'Go gentle gales' (see II.i.212) is a reference to a pastoral written by Sheridan's friend Halhead; 'purling stream' airs (see II.i.208–9) recalls Sheridan's own play-adaptation of Goldsmith's *The Vicar of Wakefield* in which 'it would be better' says Moses Primrose, 'if you would take a little care of my sister and not let her be filling her head [with] novels. I never knew any good come of such stuf[f], they get their hands so plaguy full of pu[r]ling streams and dying swain'.[72]

Events in Sheridan's life, in particular, fed into the story. Thomas, the coachman, is probably a reference to Sheridan himself who once disguised as a coachman in order to meet Elizabeth.[73] The constantly enraged Sir Anthony recalls Sheridan's own father, Thomas, who writes to his son: 'How could you be so wrong-headed as to commence cold bathing at such a season of the year, and I suppose without any preparation too?'[74] More generally, the obsession with words, meaning and pedantry in the play reflects the fact that Sheridan's father wrote a dictionary and several tracts on education. The opinions Sir Anthony expresses about women and reading, meanwhile, appear to come from Sheridan's maternal grandfather who tried to prevent Sheridan's mother from learning to read, fearing a 'multiplication of love letters, or the scarcely less dangerous interchange of sentiment in the confidential effusion of female correspondence'.[75]

Some references in *The Rivals* are in-jokes. Foote's *The Maid of Bath* contains a scene in which Kitty Linnet (a lightly fictionalised version of Elizabeth Linley before she married Sheridan – see 'Author' below) is enjoined by her mother to marry an old but wealthy man: 'Would you refuse an estate, because it happen'd to be a little encumber'd?'[76] This, after an interesting gender change, becomes Sir Anthony's statement to Jack that an estate must be purchased with 'the livestock' (II.i.377). Jack is put in the same position as many women, and specifically in the position of Kitty/Elizabeth: he is told to marry without choice, a parody that epitomizes the ridiculous nature of arranged marriages.

---

[71] Quoted in Morwood, p. 32.
[72] O'Toole, p. 90; quoted in Auburn, *Sheridan's Comedies*, p. 53.
[73] Worth, p. 120.
[74] Letter of 7 December 1771 in Moore, p. 44.
[75] Morwood, p. 4.
[76] Samuel Foote, *The Maid of Bath* (1778), p. 23.

The title 'The Rivals' was instantly misunderstood, as Sheridan must have intended. It strongly implied that the play would explore the recent events of Sheridan's past; the Town and Country Magazine assumed that the play would 'have a close connexion with a certain affair at Bath in which the celebrated Miss Linley (now Mrs. Sheridan) was the subject of rivalship'.[77] In fact, The Rivals did not tell the story of Sheridan's elopement with Elizabeth Linley and contest with Mathews – and yet it contains all the elements that make up that tale. It includes parental dictatorship, secret liaisons, rivalry, and duels. And its four male characters – an Irishman, a calculating lover, a petulant lover, a rustic trying to turn gentleman – are all aspects of Sheridan himself. But echoing past experience, as Purdy points out, 'does not make [The Rivals] autobiography'.[78] The play is founded on Sheridan's life – without being about it.

Author

'The Fates warr'd with Reason, when Sheridan sprung, / Like a fungus erect from Hibernian dung' wrote one satirist, referring to Sheridan's habitual bad luck, and his Irish origin.[79] Richard Brinsley Sheridan was born in Dublin on 30 October 1751, and was christened Thomas, after his father. He lived in Dublin for the first three years of his life and intermittently from then on until 1759; as an adult he never returned to Ireland, but felt linked with the country for the rest of his life. Between 1759 and 1762 Richard lived with his family in London, but his actor father Thomas and actress mother Frances were struggling with a growing family and little money. They sent Sheridan to Harrow school, where, impoverished and away from his parents, he was 'a very low-spirited boy, much given to crying when alone'.[80] He made one good friend at school, N. B. Halhead, with whom he wrote his first literary pieces.

When Richard was fourteen, his mother, whom he had not seen for two years, died. But it was not until he was seventeen that Sheridan was finally invited to join his father, brother and sisters. The family moved to Bath, for Thomas had given over the stage to become a teacher of elocution and believed that he would find more paying pupils outside London. Richard became a drudge – a 'rhetorical usher' for a tyrannical father. The idealised

---

[77] Quoted in R. Crompton Rhodes, The Plays & Poems of Richard Brinsley Sheridan (Oxford, 1928), p. 7.
[78] Purdy, xliv.
[79] Anthony Pasquin, pseud. (actually John Williams), The Children of Thespis (1787), p. 13.
[80] Quoted Morwood, p. 8.

version of family life that informs his writing and political speeches may reflect what he wanted throughout his life but never had.

In Bath, Sheridan first made acquaintance with the Linley family, who taught music and also gave concerts. The eldest Linley daughter, Elizabeth (b. 1754), was a singer with an ethereal voice and extraordinary beauty. Richard's brother Charles fell in love with Elizabeth, as did Richard's friend Halhead. In love with her too was an elderly man, Walter Long, with whom Elizabeth's money-hungry father tried to arrange a match. Shortly afterwards Samuel Foote wrote a play, *The Maid of Bath*, about Elizabeth's conquests. Amongst its characters was 'Major Racket' based on Captain Thomas Mathews, a married man who hounded Elizabeth. In reality, Elizabeth, only sixteen years of age, was unable to cope. She turned to Sheridan for help, and he arranged for her to go to France and settle in a convent. He accompanied her there, and married her on the way. Hearing the rumours, Mathews attacked Sheridan in *The Bath Chronicle*; Sheridan returned to England where he fought and won a duel with Mathews. When Mathews retracted the apology that had been beaten out of him, the two fought another duel in which Sheridan almost died.

Thomas Sheridan tried to dissolve his son's marriage: it had been made when the couple were under age and seems to have been unconsummated. He sent Richard to London, away from Elizabeth, to study law. In London Sheridan, now of age, married his Elizabeth again in a ceremony to which his father was not invited. Deciding it was undignified for a gentleman to let his wife earn her living from singing, Sheridan searched for a profitable career – and settled, first, on writing plays, starting with *The Rivals*. When the play was, eventually, successful, Sheridan followed it by *St Patrick's Day* (1775), *The Duenna* (1775), *The School for Scandal* (1777); much later he wrote *The Critic* (1789) and *Pizarro* (1799).

Though famous early on in his career as a playwright, Richard had always looked down on the theatre and begged his father-in-law not to let Elizabeth's sister take to the stage. In 1780 he turned his interests largely to politics, becoming MP for Stafford, a position he held until 1806. The rest of his life was spent divided between affairs of state and affairs of the stage. He was a radical Whig and follower of Charles James Fox; he was one of the best speakers in the House of Commons, making famous speeches in opposition to the war in America and attacking the slave trade. In the Regency Crisis of 1788, he was principal adviser to the Prince of Wales.

His money, however, was in the theatre. He became manager and part-owner of Drury Lane in 1776, and rebuilt the theatre in 1793–4 as an investment. In 1809, Drury Lane burned down, consuming Sheridan's profits in its flames. Sheridan is said to have watched its demise from the tavern opposite, saying 'A man may surely be allowed to take a glass of wine by his own fireside'.[81] Throughout his life money was a problem: his elder son once observed that Sheridan had every right to be known as O'Sheridan (the family's original Irish name), 'since he owed everybody'.[82]

Sheridan was regularly unfaithful to his wife, though he was heartbroken when she died in 1792. He married Esther Ogle in 1795, another unhappy and unsuccessful match. By 1807 Sheridan, now a chronic drunkard, had lost the parliamentary seat of Westminster for which he had left Stafford in 1806. He sat for Ilchester until 1812, when he contested again for his Stafford seat, and lost it. He was now liable to be arrested for debt, having paid out for the unsuccessful political contests of both himself and his son, and lost the theatre. He pawned his books, sold his furniture and died in 1816 'absolutely undone and broken-hearted'.[83] He was buried in Westminster Abbey.

[81] Quoted Morwood, p. 169.
[82] Ayling, p. 16.
[83] Sheridan, *Letters*, III, 343.

EDITIONS

Purdy. R. L., ed., Sheridan, *The Rivals, A Comedy, edited from the Larpent MS* (Oxford, 1935)

Price, Cecil, ed., Sheridan, *The Letters*, 3 vols (Oxford, 1966)

Price, Cecil, ed., Sheridan, *The Dramatic Works*, 2 vols (Oxford, 1973)

Cordner, Michael, ed., Richard Sheridan, *The School for Scandal and Other Plays* (Oxford, 1998)

STAGING

Auburn, Mark S., 'The Pleasures of Sheridan's *The Rivals*: A Critical Study in the Light of Stage History', *Modern Philology*, 72 (1975), pp. 256–71

Auburn, Mark S., 'Theatre in the age of Garrick and Sheridan' in *Sheridan Studies* ed. James Morwood and David Crane (Cambridge, 1995)

Hogan, C. B., *The London Stage Part V: 1776–1800* (Carbondale, Illinois, 1968)

Stern, Tiffany, *Rehearsal from Shakespeare to Sheridan* (Oxford, 2000)

BIBLIOGRAPHIES AND CRITICAL STUDIES

Auburn, Mark S., *Sheridan's Comedies* (Lincoln and London, 1977)

Ayling, Stanley, *A Portrait of Sheridan* (London, 1985)

Davison, Peter, ed., *Sheridan: Comedies Casebook* (London, 1986)

Durant, Jack D., *Richard Brinsley Sheridan* (Boston, 1975)

Hogan, Robert, 'Plot, Character, and Comic Language in Sheridan' in *Comedy from Shakespeare to Sheridan* ed. A. R. Braunmuller and J. C. Bulman (Newark, 1986)

Kaul, A. N., *The Action of English Comedy* (Oxford, 2001)

Leff, Leonard J., 'Sheridan and Sentimentalism' in *Sheridan: Comedies Casebook* ed. Peter Davison (London, 1986)

Loftis, John, *Sheridan and the Drama of Georgian England* (Oxford, 1976)

Macklin, Susan, ed., *The Rivals* (Harlow, 1985)

Morwood, James and David Crane, eds, *Sheridan Studies* (Cambridge, 1995)

Morwood, James, *The Life and Works of Richard Brinsley Sheridan* (Edinburgh, 1985)

O'Toole, Fintan, *A Traitor's Kiss: The Life of Richard Brinsley Sheridan* (London, 1997)

Rhodes, Crompton, *Harlequin Sheridan* (Oxford, 1933)

Ricks, Christopher, 'Word Making and Mistaking' in *The State of the Language* ed. Christopher Ricks and Leonard Michaels (London, 1990)

Rowe, Jeremy, *The Rivals by Richard Sheridan* (Basingstoke, 1986)

Rodway, Alan, 'Goldsmith and Sheridan: Satirists of Sentiment' in *Renaissance and Modern Essays* ed. G. R. Hibbard (London, 1966)

Taylor, Richard C., '"Future Retrospection": Rereading Sheridan's Reviewers' in *Sheridan Studies* ed. James Morwood and David Crane (Cambridge, 1995)

Wiesenthal, Christine S., 'Representation and Experimentation in the Major Comedies of Richard Brinsley Sheridan', *Eighteenth Century Studies* 25 (1992) 309–330

Worth, Katharine, *Sheridan and Goldsmith* (London, 1992)

THE

RIVALS,

A

COMEDY.

As it is ACTED at the

Theatre-Royal in Covent-Garden.

LONDON:

Printed for John Wilkie, No. 71, St. Paul's Church-Yard.

MDCCLXXV.

PREFACE

A preface to a play seems generally to be considered as a kind of closet-prologue in which – if his piece has been successful – the author solicits that indulgence from the reader which he had before experienced from the audience. But as the scope and immediate object of a play is to please a mixed assembly in *representation* – whose judgment, in the theatre at least, is decisive – its degree of reputation is usually as determined as public, before it can be prepared for the cooler tribunal of the study. Thus any farther solicitude on the part of the writer becomes unnecessary at least, if not an intrusion; and if the piece *has* been condemned in the performance, I fear an address to the closet, like an appeal to posterity, is constantly regarded as the procrastination of a suit from a consciousness of the weakness of the cause. From these considerations, the following comedy would certainly have been submitted to the reader without any further introduction than what it had in the representation, but that its success has probably been founded on a circumstance which the author is informed has not before attended a theatrical trial, and which consequently ought not to pass unnoticed.

I need scarcely add that the circumstance alluded to was the withdrawing of the piece to remove those imperfections in the first representation which were too

5

10

15

20

25

2 *closet-prologue* a prologue to be read in a 'closet' or study (rather than acted in performance)

6 *representation* performance

9 *cooler tribunal of the study* more rational (because less heated) judgement of the reader at home. Sheridan describes the audience's judgement using legal phraseology throughout; the theme is continued in the stage's prologue that follows.

14 *suit* lawsuit

20–1 *the author . . . trial* Sheridan's theme of knowing little about the theatre (unlikely given that his father was an actor and his mother a playwright) is first introduced here. He claims to have been 'informed' that plays are not usually revised after their first performances; in fact first performance revision happened regularly.

24 *the withdrawing of the piece* The play was withdrawn after its first unsuccessful performance on 17 January 1775; it was then revised and had a second performance eleven days later.

obvious to escape reprehension, and too numerous
to admit of a hasty correction. There are few writers, I
believe, who, even in the fullest consciousness of error,
do not wish to palliate the faults which they acknowledge;
and, however trifling the performance, to second their   30
confession of its deficiencies by whatever plea seems
least disgraceful to their ability. In the present instance, it
cannot be said to amount either to candour or modesty in
me, to acknowledge an extreme inexperience and want
of judgment on matters in which, without guidance from   35
practice, or spur from success, a young man should
scarcely boast of being an adept. If it be said that, under
such disadvantages, no one should attempt to write a play,
I must beg leave to dissent from the position, while the
first point of experience that I have gained on the subject   40
is a knowledge of the candour and judgment with which
an impartial public distinguishes between the errors of
inexperience and incapacity, and the indulgence which it
shows even to a disposition to remedy the defects of either.
It were unnecessary to enter into any farther extenuation   45
of what was thought exceptionable in this play, but
that it has been said that the managers should have
prevented some of the defects before its appearance to the
public and, in particular, the uncommon length of the piece
as represented the first night. It were an ill return for the   50
most liberal and gentlemanly conduct on their side to
suffer any censure to rest where none was deserved.
Hurry in writing has long been exploded as an excuse
for an author; however, in the dramatic line, it may
happen that both an author and a manager may wish to   55
fill a chasm in the entertainment of the public with a
hastiness not altogether culpable. The season was advanced
when I first put the play into Mr Harris's hands; it was at
that time at least double the length of any acting comedy.
I profited by his judgment and experience in the curtailing   60
of it till, I believe, his feeling for the vanity of a young

29 *palliate* excuse, mitigate
34 *extreme inexperience* Sheridan wrote *The Rivals*, his first play, when he was 23.
46 *exceptionable* objectionable
53 *exploded* discredited
58 *Mr Harris* Thomas Harris, the manager of Covent Garden Theatre

author got the better of his desire for correctness, and he
left many excrescences remaining because he had assisted
in pruning so many more. Hence, though I was not
uninformed that the acts were still too long, I flattered   65
myself that, after the first trial, I might with safer
judgment proceed to remove what should appear to have
been most dissatisfactory. Many other errors there were
which might, in part, have arisen from my being by no
means conversant with plays in general, either in reading   70
or at the theatre. Yet I own that, in one respect, I did not
regret my ignorance, for as my first wish in attempting a
play was to avoid every appearance of plagiary, I thought
I should stand a better chance of effecting this from being
in a walk which I had not frequented, and where,   75
consequently, the progress of invention was less likely to
be interrupted by starts of recollection. For on subjects on
which the mind has been much informed, invention is slow
of exerting itself. Faded ideas float in the fancy like half-
forgotten dreams, and the imagination in its fullest   80
enjoyments becomes suspicious of its offspring and doubts
whether it has created or adopted.

With regard to some particular passages which, on
the first night's representation, seemed generally disliked,
I confess that if I felt any emotion of surprise at the   85
disapprobation, it was not that they were disapproved of,
but that I had not before perceived that they deserved it.
As some part of the attack on the piece was begun too
early to pass for the sentence of *judgment*, which is ever
tardy in condemning, it has been suggested to me that   90
much of the disapprobation must have arisen from
virulence of malice rather than severity of criticism. But
as I was more apprehensive of there being just grounds
to excite the latter than conscious of having deserved the
former, I continue not to believe that probable, which I   95

---

66 *first trial* First performances were known as 'trials' as they were the occasions on which
a play was judged by the audience; here, in stating his original intention to cut the
play in the light of audience-criticism, Sheridan contradicts his earlier statement
(l. 20–1).

69–71 *by no means . . . theatre* The Rivals in fact has many obvious antecedents both in terms
of plot and lines. See 'Sources' in Introduction.

am sure must have been unprovoked. However, if it was
so, and I could even mark the quarter from whence it
came, it would be ungenerous to retort: for no passion
suffers more than malice from disappointment. For my
own part, I see no reason why the author of a play should   100
not regard a first night's audience, as a candid and
judicious friend attending, in behalf of the public, at his
last rehearsal. If he can dispense with flattery, he is sure
at least of sincerity, and even though the annotation be
rude, he may rely upon the justness of the comment.   105
Considered in this light, that audience, whose *fiat* is
essential to the poet's claim, whether his object be fame
or profit, has surely a right to expect some deference to
its opinion, from principles of politeness at least, if not
from gratitude.   110
As for the little puny critics, who scatter their
peevish strictures in private circles and scribble at every
author who has the eminence of being unconnected
with them, as they are usually spleen-swollen from a
vain idea of increasing their consequence, there will   115
always be found a petulance and illiberality in their
remarks, which should place them as far beneath the
notice of a gentleman, as their original dullness had sunk
them from the level of the most unsuccessful author.
It is not without pleasure that I catch at an   120
opportunity of justifying myself from the charge of
intending any national reflection in the character of Sir
Lucius O'Trigger. If any gentlemen opposed the piece
from that idea, I thank them sincerely for their
opposition; and if the condemnation of this comedy,   125
however misconceived the provocation, could have added
one spark to the decaying flame of national attachment to
the country supposed to be reflected on, I should have
been happy in its fate; and might with truth have boasted,
that it had done more real service in its failure, than the   130

102–3 *judicious friend . . . last rehearsal* The theme of critics at a rehearsal was of continual interest to Sheridan and two of his plays concern it: *Ixion* and *The Critic*.

106 *fiat* pronouncement (from the Latin 'let it be done')

114 *spleen-swollen* filled with 'spleen' or spite

122 *national reflection* Sheridan's portrayal of Sir Lucius was seen to be an attack on the Irish
nation.

successful morality of a thousand stage-novels will ever
effect.

It is usual, I believe, to thank the performers in a
new play, for the exertion of their several abilities. But
where, as in this instance, their merit has been so striking   135
and uncontroverted as to call for the warmest and truest
applause from a number of judicious audiences, the
poet's after-praise comes like the feeble acclamation of a
child to close the shouts of a multitude. The conduct,
however, of the principals in a theatre cannot be so   140
apparent to the public. I think it, therefore, but justice to
declare that from this theatre – the only one I can speak
of from experience – those writers who wish to try the
dramatic line, will meet with that candour and liberal
attention which are generally allowed to be better   145
calculated to lead genius into excellence, than either the
precepts of judgment, or the guidance of experience.

THE AUTHOR

131   *stage-novels* the variety of stage-plays that, like the novels that Lydia reads in *The Rivals*,
      are sentimental
136   *uncontroverted* indisputable

PROLOGUE

BY THE AUTHOR

Spoken by Mr Woodward and Mr Quick

Enter [*Woodward the*] SERGEANT AT LAW, *and* [*Quick the*]
ATTORNEY [DIBBLE]

SERGEANT
What's here? A vile cramp hand! I cannot see
Without my spectacles.
ATTORNEY [*Aside*]   He means his fee.
[*To* SERGEANT] Nay, Mr Sergeant, good sir, try again.
(*Gives money* [*to* SERGEANT])
SERGEANT
The scrawl improves!   ([ATTORNEY *gives*] *more* [*money*])
O come, 'tis pretty plain.
Hey – how's this? Dibble! Sure it cannot be!   5
A poet's brief! A poet and a fee!
ATTORNEY
Yea, sir! Though *you* without reward, I know,
Would gladly plead the muses' cause –
SERGEANT   So, so!
ATTORNEY
And if the fee offends, your wrath should fall
On me –
SERGEANT Dear Dibble, no offence at all!   10
ATTORNEY
Some sons of Phoebus in the courts we meet –
SERGEANT
And fifty sons of Phoebus in the Fleet!

---

0 s.d. 1 *Woodward* played Jack Absolute, *Quick* was Bob Acres
0 s.d. 2–3 SERGEANT AT LAW *and* ATTORNEY barrister and solicitor. In this prologue the
  Attorney bribes the Sergeant to plead the case for the poet (Sheridan) who is on 'trial'
  in front of the audience. First performances were often thought of as 'trials' because they
  were occasions on which the audience could accept ('approve') or condemn ('damn')
  the play.
6 *brief* a concise statement of the client's (in this instance, the poet's) case
11 *sons of Phoebus* poets (Phoebus Apollo was the god of poetry)
12 *Fleet* a debtors' prison in London

[38]

ATTORNEY

    Nor pleads he worse who with a decent sprig
    Of bays adorns his legal waste of wig.

SERGEANT

    Full-bottomed heroes thus, on signs, unfurl   15
    A leaf of laurel in a grove of curl!
    Yet tell your client, that, in adverse days,
    This wig is warmer than a bush of bays.

ATTORNEY

    Do you then, sir, my client's place supply,
    Profuse of robe, and prodigal of tie.   20
    Do you, with all those blushing powers of face
    And wonted bashful, hesitating grace,
    Rise in the court, and flourish on the case.   *Exit*

SERGEANT

    For practice, then, suppose – this brief will show it –
    Me, Sergeant Woodward, council for the poet.   25
    Used to the ground, I know 'tis hard to deal
    With this dread *court,* from whence there's *no appeal;*
    No *tricking* here to blunt the edge of *law,*
    Or, damned in *equity,* escape by *flaw;*
    But, *judgment* given, your sentence must remain –   30
    No *writ* of *error* lies to *Drury Lane!*
    Yet, when so kind you seem, 'tis past dispute
    We gain some favour, if not *costs of suit.*
    No spleen is here! I see no hoarded fury:
    I think I never faced a milder jury!   35

14 *bays* laurel-wreath symbolising distinction in the poetic arts
15 *Full-bottomed heroes* eminent judges and lawyers who wore heavy shoulder-length wigs
16 *A leaf . . . curl* a leaf of (poetic) bays hidden amongst the curls of the (legal) wig. Sheri-
    dan had initially gone to London to study law at the Middle Temple; this passage may
    also refer to his change of profession.
18 *wig . . . bays* it is financially better to be a lawyer than a poet
20 *tie* tie-wig (a wig in which the hair is gathered at the back)
22 *wonted* usual
23 *flourish* be eloquent
29 *damned in equity, escape by flaw* having been condemned by one kind of law, escape by
    exploiting a mistake in the proceedings
31 *Drury Lane* If Covent Garden theatre, where *The Rivals* is being performed, damns the
    play, it cannot be re-tried by the audience at the other theatre, Drury Lane.
33 *costs of suit* the legal cost of the court proceeding; also the cost of staging the performance

Sad else our plight! Where frowns are transportation,
A hiss the gallows, and a groan, damnation!
But such the public candour, without fear
My client waives all *right of challenge* here.
No newsman from *our* session is dismissed,   40
Nor wit nor critic *we* scratch off the list.
His faults can never hurt another's ease;
His crime, at worst, a *bad attempt* to please.
Thus, all respecting, he appeals to all,
And by the general voice will *stand* or *fall*.   [*Exit*]   45

36 *transportation* Criminals could be sentenced to permanent exile to the colonies.
39 *waives all right of challenge* dismisses the right to send away members of the jury who
may be biased

PROLOGUE

BY THE AUTHOR

Spoken on the tenth night, by Mrs Bulkley

Granted our cause, our suit and trial o'er,
The worthy Sergeant need appear no more.
In pleading, I a different client choose:
He served the poet; I would serve the muse.
Like him, I'll try to merit your applause,   5
A female counsel in a female's cause.
Look on this form, where humour, quaint and sly,
Dimples the cheek and points the beaming eye;
Where gay invention seems to boast its wiles
In amorous hint, and half-triumphant smiles,   10
While her light mask or covers satire's strokes,
Or hides the conscious blush her wit provokes.
Look on her well: does she seem formed to teach?
Should you *expect* to hear this lady – preach?
Is grey experience suited to her youth?   15
Do solemn sentiments become that mouth?
Bid her be grave, those lips should rebel prove
To every theme that slanders mirth or love.
Yet thus adorned with every graceful art
To charm the fancy and yet reach the heart,   20
Must we displace her? And, instead, advance
The goddess of the woeful countenance,
The sentimental muse! Her emblems view:
The Pilgrim's Progress, and a sprig of rue!

0   s.d. *Mrs Bulkley* took the part of Julia
3   *In pleading* British Library Add. MS 58277, fo. 138 and ed. (*In pleasing* 76)
7   *this form* points at the figure of Comedy in Covent Garden Theatre
11 *mask or* British Library Add. MS 58277, fo. 138 and ed. (masks or 76)
12 *Or* British Library Add. MS 58277, fo. 138 and ed. (and 76)
11–12 *or . . . or* either . . . or
13–14 Probably a parody of Garrick's prologue to *The False Delicacy*, spoken by 'Tom Fool'. See
       The Poetical Works of David Garrick, Esq (1785), 241: 'Do, ladies, look upon me – nay, no
       simp'ring: / Think you this face was ever made for whimp'ring?'
23 *The sentimental muse* The sentimental muse must not be allowed to displace the muse
    of pure comedy.
24 *The Pilgrim's Progress* by John Bunyan (1678), a moral and moralising allegory
    rue an emblem of sorrow, worn at funerals

View her – too chaste to look like flesh and blood –   25
Primly portrayed on emblematic wood!
There fixed in usurpation should she stand,
She'll snatch the dagger from her sister's hand,
And, having made her votaries *weep a flood*,
Good heaven! – she'll end her comedies in blood,   30
Bid Harry Woodward break poor Dunstall's crown,
Imprison Quick, and knock Ned Shuter down,
While sad Barsanti, weeping o'er the scene,
Shall stab herself, or poison Mrs Green!
Such dire encroachments to prevent in time   35
Demands the critic's voice, the poet's rhyme.
Can our light scenes add strength to holy laws?
Such puny patronage but hurts the cause.
Fair virtue scorns our feeble aid to ask,
And moral truth disdains the trickster's mask.   40
For here their favourite stands, whose brow, severe
And sad, claims youth's respect, and pity's tear,
Who – when oppressed by foes her worth creates –
Can point a poniard at the guilt she hates.

26 *emblematic wood* The suggestion is that there was also a wooden pictorial representation of the sentimental muse at Covent Garden.
27 *There . . . stand* 'If she stands fixed there in her wrongful eminence'
28 *snatch . . . hand* wrest the dagger from Tragedy, her sister
29 *votaries* followers
27–30 The suggestion is that 'sentimental' plays will soon take on tragic overtones.
31–4 Henry Woodward, John Dunstall, John Quick, Edward ('Ned') Shuter, Jane Barsanti,
Jane (Mrs Henry) Green all performed in the first production of *The Rivals*
41 *For here* points at the figure of Tragedy in Covent Garden Theatre
44 *poniard* small dagger

DRAMATIS PERSONAE

MEN

SIR ANTHONY ABSOLUTE	Mr Shuter
CAPT[AIN JACK] ABSOLUTE	Mr Woodward
FAULKLAND	Mr Lewis
[BOB] ACRES	Mr Quick
SIR LUCIUS O'TRIGGER	Mr Clinch
FAG	Mr Lee Lewes
DAVID	Mr Dunstall
COACHMAN [THOMAS]	Mr Fearon

WOMEN

MRS MALAPROP	Mrs Green
LYDIA LANGUISH	Miss Barsanti
JULIA MELVILLE	Mrs Bulkley
LUCY	Mrs Lessingham

MAID, BOY, SERVANTS, &c.

SCENE, *Bath*

Time of action, within one day

1   *ABSOLUTE* inflexible and arbitrary; precise in speech. *Mr Shuter* Edward Shuter 1728 (or later)?–1776

2   *Mr Woodward* Henry Woodward 1714–1777

3   *FAULKLAND* Faulkland's first name may be Jack. See V.iii.279 and note. *Mr Lewis* Philip Lewis d. 1791

4   *ACRES* named for the land he owns, as is his residence, Clod Hall. *Mr Quick* John Quick 1748–1831

5   *O'TRIGGER* named for his love of gun-fighting (Irishmen were said to be addicted to duelling), as is the name of his residence, Blunderbuss Hall. *Mr Clinch* John Lee 1725–1781 played the role successfully from the second performance onwards; the first, unsuccessful, O'Trigger was Lawrence Clinch d. 1812

6   *FAG* a drudge. *Mr Lee Lewes* Charles Lee Lewes 1740–1803

7   *Mr Dunstall* John Dunstall 1717–1778

8   *Mr Fearon* James Fearon 1746–1789

9   *MALAPROP* from the French *mal à propos*, inappropriate. *Mrs Green* Mrs Henry Green, Jane, née Hippisley 1719–1791

10   *LANGUISH* wasting away with desire. *Miss Barsanti* Jane Barsanti d. 1795

11   *Mrs Bulkley* Mrs George Bulkley, Mary, née Wilford, later Mrs Ebenezer Barrisford, 1748–1792

12   *Mrs Lessingham* Jane Lessingham 1739?–1783

15   *within one day* 76 (five hours 75)

[43]

The Rivals

Act I, Scene i

A street in Bath

[THOMAS, *a*] *coachman crosses the stage. Enter*
FAG, *looking after him*

FAG

[*Calls*] What! Thomas! [*Aside*] Sure 'tis he! [*Calls*] What!
Thomas! Thomas!

THOMAS

Hey! Od's life! Mr Fag! Give us your hand, my old
fellow-servant.

FAG

Excuse my glove, Thomas. I'm devilish glad to see you,   5
my lad. Why, my prince of charioteers, you look as
hearty – but who the deuce thought of seeing you in Bath?

THOMAS

Sure, Master, Madam Julia, Harry, Mrs Kate, and the
postillion be all come!

FAG

Indeed!   10

THOMAS

Ay, Master thought another fit of the gout was coming
to make him a visit, so he'd a mind to gi't the slip, and –
whip – we were all off at an hour's warning.

---

0   s.d. *A street* This conversation takes place on the street where Mrs Malaprop and Lydia
    Languish are staying (l. 97). Confusingly, the address of the two ladies is identified as 'the
    Grove' in the edition of 75, and as North Parade in the Larpent manuscript; in 76 the
    address is not identified.
3   *Od's life* 'God's life' – a mild expletive
5   Thomas asks for a hand, Fag pointedly draws attention to his gloves. Throughout the
    scene Thomas's honest simplicity will be contrasted with the affectations Fag has acquired
    in Bath.
7   *deuce* devil
9   *postillion* rider of one of the front horses of a carriage or post-chaise
11 *Ay* Yes
    gout popularly thought to be alleviated by spa water – hence the trip to Bath

FAG

Ay, ay! Hasty in everything, or it would not be Sir
Anthony Absolute!   15

THOMAS

But tell us, Mr Fag, how does young Master? Od, Sir
Anthony will stare to see the Captain here!

FAG

I do not serve Captain Absolute now.

THOMAS

Why sure!

FAG

At present I am employed by Ensign Beverley.   20

THOMAS

I doubt, Mr Fag, you ha'n't changed for the better.

FAG

I have not changed, Thomas.

THOMAS

No! Why, didn't you say you had left young Master?

FAG

No. Well, honest Thomas, I must puzzle you no farther.
Briefly then: Captain Absolute and Ensign Beverley are   25
one and the same person.

THOMAS

The devil they are!

FAG

So it is indeed, Thomas; and the *Ensign* half of my master
being on guard at present, the *Captain* has nothing to do
with me.   30

THOMAS

So, so! What, this is some freak, I warrant! Do tell us, Mr
Fag, the meaning o't. You know I ha' trusted you.

FAG

You'll be secret, Thomas?

THOMAS

As a coach-horse.

---

20   *Ensign* most junior rank of commissioned officer in the infantry
21   *I doubt . . . better* 'I fear you have not changed for the better'
31   *freak* whim
32   *trusted you* confided in you
34   *coach-horse* Thomas's language is full of coaching imagery. See also ll. 55, 62, 84–5.

FAG

Why – then the cause of all this is L,O,V,E. Love,   35
Thomas, who – as you may get read to you – has been
a masquerader ever since the days of Jupiter.

THOMAS

Ay, ay, I guessed there was a lady in the case. But pray,
why does your master pass only for ensign? Now if he
had shammed general indeed –   40

FAG

Ah, Thomas, there lies the mystery o'the matter.
Hark'ee, Thomas. My master is in love with a lady of a
very singular taste; a lady who likes him better as a
half-pay ensign than if she knew he was son and heir to
Sir Anthony Absolute, a baronet of three thousand a   45
year!

THOMAS

That is an odd taste indeed! But has she got the stuff, Mr
Fag? Is she rich, hey?

FAG

Rich! Why, I believe she owns half the stocks! Zounds,
Thomas, she could pay the national debt as easily as I   50
could my washerwoman! She has a lapdog that eats out
of gold, she feeds her parrot with small pearls, and all
her thread-papers are made of banknotes!

---

36   *as you may get read to you* Fag implies Thomas cannot read.
37   *Jupiter* king of gods according to Roman mythology, who took on a variety of disguises
     in order to seduce women. In the Larpent manuscript 'Jupiter' is rendered 'Juniper' and
     the source for the story 'Ovid's Meat-for-Horses' [Ovid's *Metamorphosis*] revealing Fag's
     ignorance. In revisions, Sheridan seems to have tried to confine Malapropisms to Mrs
     Malaprop.
42   *Hark'ee* 'Hark ye': listen
43   *singular* peculiar, odd
44   *half-pay ensign* i.e. poor: ensigns not in active service were given half the usual salary as
     a retainer.
45   *of* 76 (with 75)
45–6 *baronet of three thousand a year* 'Baronet' is the lowest title that can be inherited; Sir
     Anthony is financially comfortable but is not wealthy.
49   *stocks* money lent to the government for interest – a way of funding the national debt
     Zounds a corruption of 'God's wounds' – a mild expletive
50   *easily* 76 (easy 75)
53   *thread-papers* strips of paper folded in creases around which different skeins of thread
     were wound

THOMAS

Bravo! Faith! Od! I warrant she has a set of thousands at
least. But does she draw kindly with the Captain?   55

FAG

As fond as pigeons.

THOMAS

May one hear her name?

FAG

Miss Lydia Languish. But there is an old tough aunt in
the way – though, by the bye, she has never seen my
master, for he got acquainted with Miss while on a   60
visit in Gloucestershire.

THOMAS

Well, I wish they were once harnessed together in
matrimony. But pray, Mr Fag, what kind of a place is this
Bath? I ha' heard a deal of it. Here's a mort o'merry-
making, hey?   65

FAG

Pretty well, Thomas, pretty well: 'tis a good lounge. In
the morning we go to the Pump Room, though neither
my master nor I drink the waters. After breakfast we
saunter on the Parades or play a game at billiards. At
night we dance, but – damn the place – I'm tired of it!   70
Their regular hours stupefy me: not a fiddle nor a card

54   *a set* a team of (usually six) horses

55   *draw kindly with* get on well with. The metaphor refers to horses pulling together in harness.

56   *pigeons* turtle doves, traditional symbols of affection

64   *mort* great quantity (dialect). Thomas speaks in a country brogue.

66   *lounge* place for lounging

  lounge. 76. (75 continues: Though at present we are, like other great assemblies, divided
  into parties, High-roomians and Low-roomians. However, for my part, I have resolved
  to stand neuter, and so I told Bob Brush at our last committee. THOMAS But what do the
  folks do here? FAG O! There are little amusements enough)

67   *Pump Room* the room in which the spa waters were dispensed and, therefore, also, the
  place where visitors generally assembled

69   *Parades* The fashionable North and South Parades of eighteenth-century Bath were wide
  paved streets parallel to one another.

71–2   *Their regular hours . . . after eleven* Balls and other public assemblies were supposed to end
  by 11 p.m. as stated in regulations laid down by Richard 'Beau' Nash, Master of Ceremonies
  at Bath from 1705 to 1761, and maintained by his successor Captain William Wade, who
  further refined the rules in 1771: 'The balls will begin as soon as possible after six o'clock,
  and finish precisely at eleven, even in the middle of a dance', *New Bath Guide*, 1777, 26.

after eleven! However, Mr Faulkland's gentleman and
I keep it up a little in private parties. I'll introduce you
there, Thomas, you'll like him much.

THOMAS

Sure I know Mr Du Peigne. You know his master is to   75
marry Madam Julia?

FAG

I had forgot. But, Thomas, you must polish a little,
indeed you must. Here now – this wig! What the devil do
you do with a *wig*, Thomas? None of the London whips
of any degree of ton wear *wigs* now.   80

THOMAS

More's the pity! More's the pity, I say. Od's life, when I
heard how the lawyers and doctors had took to their own
hair, I thought how 'twould go next. Od rabbit it! When
the fashion had got foot on the bar, I guessed 'twould
mount to the box! But 'tis all out of character, believe   85
me, Mr Fag, and – look'ee – I'll never gi' up mine. The
lawyers and doctors may do as they will.

FAG

Well, Thomas, we'll not quarrel about that.

THOMAS

Why, bless you, the gentlemen of they professions ben't
all of a mind, for in our village now, tho'ff *Jack Gauge*   90
the exciseman, has ta'en to his carrots, there's little Dick

---

72 *gentleman* (here) *valet de chambre*, personal servant
75 *Mr Du Peigne* 'He of the Comb', a French valet
77 *polish* become more fashionable, acquire finesse
78 *wig* The fashion for wearing wigs was dying by the late 1770s; it became modish to pow-
    der one's own hair instead.
79 *whips* coachmen
80 *ton* fashionableness (from the French 'ton' meaning 'style')
83 *Od rabbit it* a meaningless imprecation, perhaps a corruption of 'God rot it' or 'God drat
    it'
83–5 *When . . . box* i.e. 'When the fashion was taken on by lawyers (the Bar) I guessed it would
    be adopted by coachmen (the Box)'; continuing the coaching imagery, 'bar' can also
    mean the bar of a carriage used as a foothold in mounting to the 'box' where coachmen
    sit
86 *look'ee* 'look ye': look here! Attend!
89–90 *they . . . ben't . . . tho'ff* those . . . are not . . . though (dialect)
90–91 *Jack Gauge the exciseman* An exciseman was a customs official who measured or 'gauged'
    casks containing alcohol to determine how much duty should be levied on them.
91 *carrots* (natural) red hair

the farrier swears he'll never forsake his bob, though all
the college should appear with their own heads!

FAG

Indeed! Well said, Dick! But hold – mark! Mark, Thomas!

THOMAS

Zooks! 'Tis the Captain! Is that the lady with him?   95

FAG

No, no! That is Madam Lucy my master's mistress's maid.
They lodge at that house. But I must after him to tell him
the news.

THOMAS

Od, he's giving her money! Well, Mr Fag –

FAG

Goodbye, Thomas. I have an appointment in Gyde's   100
Porch this evening at eight. Meet me there, and we'll
make a little party.

Exeunt severally

[Act I,] Scene ii

A dressing-room in MRS MALAPROP's *lodgings*

LYDIA [LANGUISH] *sitting on a sofa with a book in her hand.*
LUCY, *as just returned from a message*

LUCY

Indeed, ma'am, I traversed half the town in search of it.
I don't believe there's a circulating library in Bath I

---

92   *farrier* blacksmith and horse doctor
     bob bob-peruke – a wig which had short ('bobbed') curls at the bottom
93   *college* college of physicians or surgeons, professional institutions to which doctors belonged
95   *Zooks!* short form of 'Gadzooks!' itself a corruption of 'God's hooks!' – a mild expletive
     usually used to express surprise or vexation
100–101 *Gyde's Porch* Mr Gyde kept the old Assembly Rooms on the Lower Walks in Bath.

1   *traversed* 76 (*transferred* 75 and Larpent). 'Transferred' makes no sense in the context.
    Sheridan seems originally to have intended several characters to use malapropisms; this
    example would have shown that Lucy, like Mrs Malaprop, aspired to a vocabulary she
    did not possess.
2   *circulating library* Booksellers at the time lent out their collection for a small fee.

ha'n't been at.

LYDIA

And could not you get *The Reward of Constancy*?

LUCY

No, indeed, ma'am.   5

LYDIA

Nor *The Fatal Connection*?

LUCY

No, indeed, ma'am.

LYDIA

Nor *The Mistakes of the Heart*?

LUCY

Ma'am, as ill luck would have it, Mr Bull said Miss
Sukey Saunter had just fetched it away.   10

LYDIA

Heigh-ho! Did you inquire for *The Delicate Distress*?

LUCY

Or *The Memoirs of Lady Woodford*? Yes indeed, ma'am.
I asked everywhere for it; and I might have brought it
from Mr Frederick's, but Lady Slattern Lounger, who
had just sent it home, had so soiled and dog's-eared it, it   15
wa'n't fit for a Christian to read.

LYDIA

Heigh-ho! Yes, I always know when Lady Slattern has
been before me. She has a most observing thumb, and, I
believe, cherishes her nails for the convenience of
making marginal notes. Well, child, what *have* you   20
brought me?

4 *The Reward of Constancy* possibly *Female Constancy; or, the History of Miss Arabella
   Waldegrave* (1769), or *The Happy Pair, or Virtue and Constancy Rewarded* (1771). Most
   books Lydia borrows from the circulating libraries in Bath are sentimental novels.

6 *The Fatal Connection* by Mrs Fogerty, 2 vols (1773)

8 *The Mistakes of the Heart* by Pierre Henri Treyssac de Vergy, 3 vols (1769)

9 *Mr Bull* Lewis Bull was a Bath bookseller whose shop was situated opposite Gyde's rooms
   on the Lower Walks.

11 *The Delicate Distress* by Elizabeth Griffith (1769)

12 *The Memoirs of Lady Woodford* written by herself (1771)

14 *Mr Frederick's* William Frederick, another Bath bookseller, kept a bookshop at 18 The Grove.

15 *dog's-eared* marked the place by turning down the corners of the pages

LUCY

O! Here ma'am! (*Taking books from under her cloak, and from her pockets*) This is *The Gordian Knot,* and this *Peregrine Pickle.* Here are *The Tears of Sensibility* and *Humphrey Clinker.* This is *The Memoirs of a Lady of Quality, Written by Herself,* and here the second volume of *The Sentimental Journey.*   25

LYDIA

Heigh-ho! What are those books by the glass?

LUCY

The great one is only *The Whole Duty of Man* – where I press a few blondes, ma'am.   30

LYDIA

Very well. Give me the sal volatile.

LUCY

Is it in a blue cover, ma'am?

LYDIA

My smelling-bottle, you simpleton!

LUCY

O, the drops! Here, ma'am.

LYDIA

Hold! Here's someone coming. Quick – see who it is.   35

Exit LUCY

23 *The Gordian Knot* by Richard Griffith (1769) was published as the second half of a four-volume set with Elizabeth Griffith's *Delicate Distress*

24 *Peregrine Pickle* by Tobias Smollett (1751) was republished in expurgated and revised form in 1758. It is unclear which version Lucy has brought.
    The Tears of Sensibility four French novels by Baculard d'Arnoud translated by John Murdoch, 2 vols (1773)

25 *Humphrey Clinker The Expedition of Humphrey Clinker* by Tobias Smollett (1771)

25–6 *The Memoirs of a Lady of Quality, Written by Herself* a detachable segment of Smollet's *Peregrine Pickle* supposed to be by Lady Vane. Lucy appears, unthinkingly, to have bought a segment of the same book twice.

27 *The Sentimental Journey* by Laurence Sterne, 2 vols (1768)

28 *glass* looking-glass, mirror

29 *The Whole Duty of Man* attributed to Richard Allestree (1659), a lengthy and popular work of piety. Its use for pressing blondes indicates that Lydia does not intend to read it.

30 *blondes* pieces of silk lace made from two threads twisted into hexagonal meshes

31 *sal volatile* ammonium carbonate, called 'sal volatile' when drunk and 'smelling salts' when sniffed; it was thought to ward off headaches or faintness

34 *Here, ma'am.* 76 (75 continues: LYDIA No note, Lucy? LUCY No indeed, ma'am, but I have seen a certain person. LYDIA What – my Beverley! Well, Lucy? LUCY O ma'am! He looks so desponding and melancholic!)

35 *Hold!* 76 (Hold Lucy! 75)

Surely I heard my cousin Julia's voice!

Enter LUCY

LUCY

Lud, ma'am, here is Miss Melville.

LYDIA

Is it possible?

Enter JULIA [MELVILLE *and exit* LUCY]

LYDIA

My dearest Julia, how delighted am I! (*Embrace*[s JULIA])
How unexpected was this happiness!   40

JULIA

True, Lydia, and our pleasure is the greater. But what has
been the matter? You were denied to me at first!

LYDIA

Ah, Julia, I have a thousand things to tell you! But first
inform me what has conjured you to Bath? Is Sir Anthony
here?   45

JULIA

He is. We are arrived within this hour, and I suppose he
will be here to wait on Mrs Malaprop as soon as he is
dressed.

LYDIA

Then, before we are interrupted, let me impart to you
some of my distress! I know your gentle nature will   50
sympathize with me, though your prudence may
condemn me! My letters have informed you of my whole
connection with Beverley – but I have lost him, Julia! My
aunt has discovered our intercourse by a note she
intercepted, and has confined me ever since! Yet – would   55

---

36 s.d. *Enter* LUCY ed. (*Re-enter Lucy* 75, 76)
38 s.d. *and exit* LUCY ed. (exit recorded in Larpent only)
39 s.d. ed. (*Embrace* 75, 76)
42 *denied* i.e. the servants told her Lydia was not receiving visitors (in fact Mrs Malaprop
    has confined Lydia to her room)
44 *conjured* brought by magical compulsion
47 *wait on* pay his respects to
47–8 *as soon as he is dressed* i.e. as soon as he has changed out of his travelling clothes into for-
    mal attire
54 *intercourse* communication, dealings

you believe it? – she has fallen absolutely in love with a
tall Irish baronet she met one night since we have been
here, at Lady Macshuffle's rout.

JULIA

You jest, Lydia!

LYDIA

No, upon my word. She really carries on a kind of   60
correspondence with him – under a feigned name, though,
till she chooses to be known to him, but it is a Delia or a
Celia, I assure you.

JULIA

Then, surely, she is now more indulgent to her niece.

LYDIA

Quite the contrary. Since she has discovered her own   65
frailty, she is become more suspicious of mine. Then I
must inform you of another plague! That odious Acres
is to be in Bath today, so that I protest I shall be teased
out of all spirits!

JULIA

Come, come, Lydia, hope the best. Sir Anthony shall use   70
his interest with Mrs Malaprop.

LYDIA

But you have not heard the worst. Unfortunately I had
quarrelled with my poor Beverley just before my aunt
made the discovery, and I have not seen him since to
make it up.   75

JULIA

What was his offence?

LYDIA

Nothing at all! But – I don't know how it was – as often
as we had been together, we had never had a quarrel, and,
somehow, I was afraid he would never give me an
opportunity. So, last Thursday, I wrote a letter to myself   80

---

58   *rout* fashionable gathering, large evening party or reception
60   *really* 76 (absolutely 75)
62–3 *a Delia or a Celia* conventional names for a mistress in love poetry and so fashionable
      in courtship
68   *teased* harassed, tormented
71   *interest* influence

to inform myself that Beverley was at that time paying
his addresses to another woman. I signed it 'your Friend
Unknown', showed it to Beverley, charged him with his
falsehood, put myself in a violent passion, and vowed I'd
never see him more.　　　　　　　　　　　　　　　　85

JULIA

And you let him depart so and have not seen him since?

LYDIA

'Twas the next day my aunt found the matter out. I
intended only to have teased him three days and a half,
and now I've lost him forever.

JULIA

If he is as deserving and sincere as you have represented　90
him to me, he will never give you up so. Yet consider,
Lydia, you tell me he is but an ensign, and you have thirty
thousand pounds!

LYDIA

But you know I lose most of my fortune if I marry
without my aunt's consent till of age; and that is what I　95
have determined to do, ever since I knew the penalty.
Nor could I love the man who would wish to wait a day
for the alternative.

JULIA

Nay, this is caprice!

LYDIA

What? Does Julia tax me with caprice? I thought her lover　100
Faulkland had inured her to it.

JULIA

I do not love even *his* faults.

LYDIA

But apropos, you have sent to him, I suppose?

JULIA

Not yet, upon my word, nor has he the least idea of my

81-2　*paying his addresses to* courting
　95　*till of age* before I come of age i.e. reach the age of twenty-one
　99　*caprice* foolishness, whimsical change of mind or conduct
　101　*inured* accustomed, made familiar with
　103　*apropos* with regard to (from the French *à propos*)
　　　sent to him sent him a missive

being in Bath. Sir Anthony's resolution was so sudden I   105
could not inform him of it.

LYDIA

Well, Julia, you are your own mistress, though under the
protection of Sir Anthony. Yet have you, for this long
year, been a slave to the caprice, the whim, the jealousy
of this ungrateful Faulkland, who will ever delay assuming   110
the right of a husband, while you suffer him to be equally
imperious as a lover.

JULIA

Nay, you are wrong entirely. We were contracted before
my   father's   death.   *That*,   and   some   consequent
embarrassments, have delayed what I know to be my   115
Faulkland's most ardent wish. He is too generous to
trifle on such a point. And, for his character, you wrong
him there too. No, Lydia, he is too proud, too noble to
be jealous; if he is captious, 'tis without dissembling; if
fretful, without rudeness. Unused to the fopperies of love,   120
he is negligent of the little duties expected from a lover –
but, being unhackneyed in the passion, his affection is
ardent and sincere, and, as it engrosses his whole soul,
he expects every thought and emotion of his mistress to
move in unison with his. Yet, though his pride calls for   125
this full return, his humility makes him undervalue those
qualities in him which would entitle him to it; and not
feeling why he should be loved to the degree he wishes,

---

105   *resolution* decision (to come to Bath)
107   *you are your own mistress* Julia is of age and therefore can chose her own husband with-
      out financial consequences. Sir Anthony remains her legal guardian, however, until she
      is married.
109   *a* 76 (the 75)
113   *contracted* formally engaged
114–5 *consequent embarrassments* subsequent impediments – the impediments being, presum-
      ably, Faulkland's temperament
116   *generous* noble
119   *captious* given to finding fault, quarrelsome
120   *fopperies* 76 (foppery 75), petty refinements
122   *unhackneyed* not very accustomed to, inexperienced
      affection 76 (love 75) That Sheridan chose to change the word in later revisions of the
      play may be significant: see the similar change to l. 132.
126   *return* reciprocation, response
127   *would* 76 (should 75)

he still suspects that he is not loved enough. This temper,
I must own, has cost me many unhappy hours, but I   130
have learned to think myself his debtor for those
imperfections which arise from the ardour of his attachment.

LYDIA

Well, I cannot blame you for defending him. But tell me
candidly, Julia, had he never saved your life, do you
think you should have been attached to him as you are?   135
Believe me, the rude blast that overset your boat was a
prosperous gale of love to him.

JULIA

Gratitude may have strengthened my attachment to
Mr Faulkland, but I loved him before he had preserved me.
Yet surely that alone were an obligation sufficient.   140

LYDIA

Obligation! Why, a water-spaniel would have done as
much! Well, I should never think of giving my heart to a
man because he could swim!

JULIA

Come, Lydia, you are too inconsiderate.

LYDIA

Nay, I do but jest. – What's here?   145

Enter LUCY *in a hurry*

LUCY

O ma'am, here is Sir Anthony Absolute just come home
with your aunt.

LYDIA

They'll not come here. – Lucy do you watch.

Exit LUCY

JULIA

Yet I must go. Sir Anthony does not know I am here, and
if we meet, he'll detain me, to show me the town. I'll take 150
another opportunity of paying my respects to Mrs

---

129   *temper* temperament
132   *attachment* 76 (love 75)
141   *water-spaniel* a variety of spaniel used as a gun-dog and trained to retrieve game-birds,
      particularly water-fowl
151   *paying my respects* making a courtesy call

Malaprop, when she shall treat me, as long as she chooses, with her select words so ingeniously *misapplied*, without being *mispronounced*.

Enter LUCY

LUCY

O lud, ma'am, they are both coming upstairs!   155

LYDIA

Well, I'll not detain you, coz. Adieu, my dear Julia. I'm sure you are in haste to send to Faulkland. There through my room you'll find another staircase.

JULIA

Adieu. (*Embrace[s* LYDIA*]*)   *Exit*

LYDIA

Here, my dear Lucy, hide these books. Quick, quick!   160
Fling *Peregrine Pickle* under the toilet! Throw *Roderick Random* into the closet! Put *The Innocent Adultery* into *The Whole Duty of Man*; thrust *Lord Aimworth* under the sofa; cram *Ovid* behind the bolster – there – put *The Man of Feeling* into your pocket! So, so! Now lay *Mrs Chapone*   165
in sight, and leave Fordyce's *Sermons* open on the table.

---

154 s.d. *Enter* LUCY ed. (*Re-enter* Lucy 75, 76)
155 *O lud* A softened form of 'Oh Lord!' – an exclamation of dismay
156 *Adieu* Goodbye (from the French)
     coz an abbreviation of 'cousin' often used generally as a term of affection
157 s.d. ed. (*Embrace* 75, 76)
161 *toilet* dressing-table
161–2 *Roderick Random* by Tobias Smollett (1748)
162 *closet* cupboard
     The Innocent Adultery a French novel by Paul Scarron, translated by Samuel Croxall in 1722
163 *Lord Aimworth* meaning *The History of Lord Aimworth, and the Honourable Charles Hart-ford, Esq. in a Series of Letters* by 'the Author of Dorinda Catesby, and Ermina', 3 vols (1773)
164 *Ovid* the Roman poet (43 BC–17 AD) famous for his love poems *Amores* ('Loves') and *Ars Amatoria* ('The Art of Love') of which there were many eighteenth-century translations
     bolster long cushion or pillow on a sofa
164–5 *The Man of Feeling* by Henry Mackenzie (1771)
165 *Mrs Chapone* wrote *Letters on the Improvement of the Mind. Addressed to a young Lady,* 2 vols (1773)
166 *Fordyce's Sermons* James Fordyce wrote *Sermons to Young Women,* 2 vols (1765) in which he inveighed against the reading of novels

LUCY

O burn it, ma'am, the hairdresser has torn away as far
as 'Proper Pride'.

LYDIA

Never mind: open at 'Sobriety'. Fling me Lord
Chesterfield's *Letters*. Now for 'em.   170

Enter MRS MALAPROP *and* SIR ANTHONY ABSOLUTE

MRS MALAPROP

There, Sir Anthony, there sits the deliberate simpleton,
who wants to disgrace her family and lavish herself on a
fellow not worth a shilling!

LYDIA

Madam, I thought you once –

MRS MALAPROP

You thought, miss! I don't know any business you have   175
to think at all: thought does not become a young woman.
But the point we would request of you is, that you will
promise to forget this fellow! To illiterate him, I say,
quite from your memory.

LYDIA

Ah, madam! Our memories are independent of our wills.   180
It is not so easy to forget.

MRS MALAPROP

But I say it is, miss; there is nothing on earth so easy as
to *forget*, if a person chooses to set about it. I'm sure I
have as much forgot your poor dear uncle as if he had
never existed – and I thought it my duty so to do; and let   185
me tell you, Lydia, these violent memories don't become
a young woman.

SIR ANTHONY

Why, sure, she won't pretend to remember what she's

---

167 *burn it* drat it
     torn away The hairdresser has taken pages from the book to make 'curl-papers', the pre-
     cursor to hair-rollers.
169–70 *Lord Chesterfield's Letters* by Philip Stanhope, fourth Earl of Chesterfield (1774)
171 *deliberate* in this context, may mean 'wary' or 'slow'
176–7 *woman. But the* 76 (woman; the 75)
178 *illiterate* for, obliterate
188 *pretend* plan, claim

ordered not! Ay, this comes of her reading!

LYDIA

What crime, madam, have I committed to be treated thus?   190

MRS MALAPROP

Now don't attempt to extirpate yourself from the matter; you know I have proof controvertible of it. But tell me, will you promise to do as you're bid? Will you take a husband of your friends' choosing?

LYDIA

Madam, I must tell you plainly, that had I no preference   195
for anyone else, the choice you have made would be my aversion.

MRS MALAPROP

What business have you, miss, with *preference* and *aversion*? They don't become a young woman; and you ought to know that – as both always wear off – 'tis   200
safest in matrimony to begin with a little *aversion*. I am sure I hated your poor dear uncle before marriage as if he'd been a blackamoor – and yet, miss, you are sensible what a wife I made! And when it pleased heaven to release me from him, 'tis unknown what tears I shed!   205
But suppose we were going to give you another choice, will you promise us to give up this Beverley?

LYDIA

Could I belie my thoughts so far as to give that promise, my actions would certainly as far belie my words.

MRS MALAPROP

Take yourself to your room! You are fit company for   210
nothing but your own ill humours.

---

189 *ordered not* ordered not to do
191 *extirpate* root out or 'exterminate': for, extricate or exculpate
192 *controvertible* for, incontrovertible
196–7 *the choice . . . aversion* 'I would hate your choice'
203 *blackamoor* black African
      sensible aware
205 *unknown what tears I shed* i.e. no one knows the number of tears I shed – a double-edged statement: she may have shed no tears at all
208 *belie* give the lie to
211 *ill humours* the 'temper' was said to be controlled by the four humours, melancholy, phlegm, blood and choler, producing people who were melancholic, phlegmatic, sanguine or choleric. Ill humour therefore means a bad temper.

LYDIA

Willingly, ma'am. I cannot change for the worse.   *Exit*

MRS MALAPROP

There's a little intricate hussy for you!

SIR ANTHONY

It is not to be wondered at, ma'am; all this is the natural
consequence of teaching girls to read. Had I a thousand   215
daughters, by heavens, I'd as soon have them taught the
black art as their alphabet!

MRS MALAPROP

Nay, nay, Sir Anthony, you are an absolute misanthropy.

SIR ANTHONY

In my way hither, Mrs Malaprop, I observed your niece's
maid coming forth from a circulating library. She had a   220
book in each hand: they were half-bound volumes, with
marble covers! From that moment I guessed how full
of duty I should see her mistress!

MRS MALAPROP

Those are vile places, indeed!

SIR ANTHONY

Madam, a circulating library in a town is as an evergreen   225
tree of diabolical knowledge! It blossoms through the
year! And depend on it, Mrs Malaprop, that they who are

---

212 s.d. *Exit* ed. (*Exit Lydia* 75, 76) Where the character who is speaking exits the
stage direction is abbreviated in this way (shorn of his/her name) throughout this
edition.

213 *intricate* perplexed or complicated: for, ingrate or perhaps obstinate
hussy cheeky girl; a playfully rude mode of addressing a woman

216 *heavens* 76 (heaven 75)

217 *black art* magic or witchcraft

218 *misanthropy* for, misanthrope (someone who hates people) or misogynist (someone who
hates women). 'Absolute misanthropy' also plays with Sir Anthony Absolute's last and
first name.

221–2 *half-bound volumes, with marble covers* volumes with the spine and corners
bound in leather and the rest supplied by boards covered in marble-pattern
paper

222 *marble* 76 (marbled 75)

225–6 *an evergreen tree of diabolical knowledge* a conflation of two passages in the Bible:
Genesis 2:17 ('But of the tree of the knowledge of good and evil, thou shalt not eat of it')
and Psalms 37:35 ('I have seen the wicked in great power, and spreading himself like a
green bay tree')

so fond of handling the leaves will long for the fruit at last.

MRS MALAPROP

Fie, fie, Sir Anthony, you surely speak laconically!

SIR ANTHONY

Why, Mrs Malaprop, in moderation now, what would   230
you have a woman know?

MRS MALAPROP

Observe me, Sir Anthony. I would by no means wish a
daughter of mine to be a progeny of learning: I don't
think so much learning becomes a young woman. For
instance, I would never let her meddle with Greek, or   235
Hebrew, or algebra, or simony, or fluxions, or paradoxes,
or such inflammatory branches of learning; neither
would it be necessary for her to handle any of your
mathematical, astronomical, diabolical instruments. But,
Sir Anthony, I would send her, at nine years old, to a   240
boarding-school, in order to learn a little ingenuity and
artifice. Then, sir, she should have a supercilious
knowledge in accounts; and as she grew up, I would have
her instructed in geometry, that she might know
something of the contagious countries. But above all,   245

228–9 *last.* (75 continues: MRS MALAPROP Well, but, Sir Anthony, your wife, Lady Absolute, was
       fond of books. SIR ANTHONY Ay, and injury sufficient they were to her, madam. But were
       I to choose another helpmate, the extent of her erudition should consist in her know-
       ing her simple letters without their mischievous combinations, and the summit of her
       science be her ability to count as far as twenty. The first, Mrs Malaprop, would enable
       her to work 'A. A.' upon my linen, and the latter would be quite sufficient to prevent her
       giving me a shirt, No. 1., and a stock, No. 2.)
229   *laconically* tersely (literally, after the manner of the Laconians or Spartans), for, ironi-
       cally
232   *Observe me* Listen to me
233   *progeny* child; for, prodigy
236   *simony* the buying and selling of church livings; for, cyclometry (the measurement of
       circles) or ciphering (computing with Arabic numbers)
       fluxions calculus in Newtonian geometry; (presumably) for, fractions
       paradoxes for, parallaxes (the distance between the actual and apparent place of any star
       viewed from earth)
237   *inflammatory* tending to inflame or over-excite
239   *diabolical* devilish
241–2 *ingenuity and artifice* can mean either 'wit and skill' or 'fraud and deceptiveness'
242   *supercilious* for, superficial
244   *geometry* for, geography
245   *contagious* for, contiguous

Sir Anthony, she should be mistress of orthodoxy, that she might not misspell, and mispronounce words so shamefully as girls usually do, and likewise that she might reprehend the true meaning of what she is saying. This, Sir Anthony, is what I would have a woman know; and I don't think there is a superstitious article in it.   250

SIR ANTHONY

Well, well, Mrs Malaprop, I will dispute the point no further with you; though I must confess that you are a truly moderate and polite arguer, for almost every third word you say is on my side of the question. But, Mrs Malaprop, to the more important point in debate – you say you have no objection to my proposal?   255

MRS MALAPROP

None, I assure you. I am under no positive engagement with Mr Acres, and as Lydia is so obstinate against him, perhaps your son may have better success.   260

SIR ANTHONY

Well, madam, I will write for the boy directly. He knows not a syllable of this yet, though I have for some time had the proposal in my head. He is at present with his regiment.

MRS MALAPROP

We have never seen your son, Sir Anthony; but I hope no objection on his side.   265

SIR ANTHONY

Objection? Let him object if he dare! No, no, Mrs Malaprop, Jack knows that the least demur puts me in a frenzy directly. My process was always very simple. In their younger days, 'twas 'Jack, do this'; if he demurred, I knocked him down, and if he grumbled at that, I always sent him out of the room.   270

246 *orthodoxy* for, orthography
249 *reprehend* for, apprehend or comprehend
251 *superstitious* for, superfluous
258–9 *I am under . . . Mr Acres* 'I am not formally committed to (marrying Lydia off to) Mr Acres'
268 *demur* hesitation
269 *process* way of proceeding

MRS MALAPROP

Ay, and the properest way, o' my conscience! Nothing
is so conciliating to young people as severity. Well, Sir
Anthony, I shall give Mr Acres his discharge, and   275
prepare Lydia to receive your son's invocations; and I
hope you will represent *her* to the Captain as an object not
altogether illegible.

SIR ANTHONY

Madam, I will handle the subject prudently. Well, I must
leave you, and let me beg you, Mrs Malaprop, to enforce   280
this matter roundly to the girl. Take my advice: keep a
tight hand. If she rejects this proposal, clap her under
lock and key; and if you were just to let the servants
forget to bring her dinner for three or four days, you
can't conceive how she'd come about!   *Exit*   285

MRS MALAPROP

Well, at any rate, I shall be glad to get her from under my
intuition. She has somehow discovered my partiality for
Sir Lucius O'Trigger. Sure, Lucy can't have betrayed me?
No, the girl is such a simpleton, I should have made her
confess it. (*Calls*) Lucy! Lucy! [*Aside*] Had she been one   290
of your artificial ones, I should never have trusted her.

Enter LUCY

LUCY

Did you call, ma'am?

MRS MALAPROP

Yes, girl. Did you see Sir Lucius while you was out?

LUCY

No, indeed, ma'am, not a glimpse of him.

MRS MALAPROP

You are sure, Lucy, that you never mentioned –   295

---

274 *conciliating* pleasing; (presumably) for, constricting or humiliating
276 *invocations* protestations of love – not a malapropism
278 *illegible* for, ineligible
281 *roundly* plainly, vigorously
287 *intuition* for, tuition
291 *artificial* for, artful
293 *you was* a common usage of the period

LUCY

O gemini! I'd sooner cut my tongue out.

MRS MALAPROP

Well, don't let your simplicity be imposed on.

LUCY

No, ma'am.

MRS MALAPROP

So, come to me presently, and I'll give you another letter
to Sir Lucius – but, mind, Lucy, if ever you betray what   300
you are entrusted with, unless it be other people's secrets
to me, you forfeit my malevolence for ever, and your
being a simpleton shall be no excuse for your locality.   *Exit*

LUCY

Ha, ha, ha! So, my dear *simplicity*, let me give you a little
respite. (*Altering her manner*) Let girls in my station be as   305
fond as they please of appearing expert and knowing in
their trusts. Commend me to a mask of *silliness*, and a
pair of sharp eyes for my own interest under it! Let me
see to what account I have turned my *simplicity* lately.
(*Looks at a paper*) 'For abetting Miss Lydia Languish in a   310
design of running away with an ensign, in money – sundry
times twelve pound twelve; gowns – five; hats, ruffles, caps,
etc. etc. – numberless! From the said ensign, within this
last month, six guineas and a half' – about a quarter's pay!
'Item, from Mrs Malaprop, for betraying the young people   315
to her' – when I found matters were likely to be
discovered – 'two guineas, and a black paduasoy. Item,
from Mr Acres, for carrying divers letters' – which I never
delivered – 'two guineas and a pair of buckles. Item, from

296 *O gemini* a mild oath, either from the constellation of Gemini, or from 'Jesu domine'; it
      survives in the exclamation 'by jimminy'
299 *presently* immediately
302 *malevolence* for, benevolence
303 *locality* for, loquacity
307 *Commend me to* Give me by choice
309 *I have* 76 (have I 75)
311 *sundry* various
314 *a quarter's pay* three months' pay
317 *paduasoy* a dress of rich corded silk; the material is named after the Italian place Padua
      and the French for silk, *soie*
318 *divers* several, various
319 *guineas* worth twenty-one shillings (£1.05)

Sir Lucius O'Trigger, three crowns, two gold pocket-pieces,   320
and a silver snuffbox!' Well done, simplicity! Yet I was
forced to make my Hibernian believe, that he was
corresponding, not with the *aunt*, but with the *niece*: for,
though not over-rich, I found he had too much pride and
delicacy to sacrifice the feelings of a gentleman to the   325
necessities of his fortune.   *Exit*

Act II, Scene i

[JACK] ABSOLUTE's *lodgings*

[JACK] ABSOLUTE *and* FAG

FAG

Sir, while I was there, Sir Anthony came in. I told him
you had sent me to inquire after his health, and to know
if he was at leisure to see you.

ABSOLUTE

And what did he say on hearing I was at Bath?

FAG

Sir, in my life I never saw an elderly gentleman more   5
astonished! He started back two or three paces, rapped
out a dozen interjectoral oaths, and asked what the
devil had brought you here!

ABSOLUTE

Well, sir, and what did you say?

FAG

O, I lied, sir. I forget the precise lie, but you may depend   10
on't, he got no truth from me. Yet, with submission, for
fear of blunders in future, I should be glad to fix what
has brought us to Bath, in order that we may lie a little

320 *crowns* worth five shillings (25p)
       gold pocket-pieces gold lucky charms – often coins that were no longer in circulation
321 *snuff box* Snuff is powdered tobacco sniffed as a stimulant; a snuff-box the ornamental
       box in which it is kept.
322 *Hibernian* Irishman

  0 s.d. 1 JACK ed. (Captain 75, 76)
       s.d. 2 JACK ed. (Captain 75, 76)
  7 *interjectoral* parenthetical, abrupt
 10 *forget* 76 (forgot 75)

consistently. Sir Anthony's servants were curious, sir, very curious indeed.   15

ABSOLUTE

You have said nothing to them?

FAG

O, not a word, sir, not a word. Mr Thomas, indeed, the coachman, whom I take to be the discreetest of whips –

ABSOLUTE

'Sdeath, you rascal! You have not trusted him!

FAG

O, *no*, sir, no, no – not a syllable, upon my veracity! He was,   20
indeed, a little inquisitive, but I was sly, sir, devilish sly!
'My master', said I, 'honest Thomas' – you know, sir, one
says *honest* to one's inferiors – 'is come to Bath to *recruit*.'
Yes, sir, I said, 'to *recruit*' – and whether for men, money,
or constitution, you know, sir, is nothing to him, nor   25
anyone else.

ABSOLUTE

Well '*recruit*' will do; let it be so.

FAG

O, sir, 'recruit' will do surprisingly. Indeed, to give the
thing an air, I told Thomas that your honour had already
enlisted five disbanded chairmen, seven minority   30
waiters, and thirteen billiard-markers.

ABSOLUTE

You blockhead, never say more than is necessary.

FAG

I beg pardon, sir, I beg pardon! But, with submission, a lie
is nothing unless one supports it. Sir, whenever I draw

---

19 '*Sdeath* an oath, from 'God's death'
20 *upon my veracity* 'truly'
24 *recruit* to enlist men for the army. But the word might also mean to find a new supply
     of money (by acquiring an heiress) or to restore health.
28–9 *to give the thing an air* to give the lie credibility
30 *enlisted* recruited, signed on
     disbanded chairmen unemployed carriers of sedan-chairs (covered chairs, for conveying
     one person, carried between horizontal poles by two men, one at each end)
30–31 *minority waiters* young, inexperienced or part-time waiters
31 *billiard-markers* billiard scorers

on my invention for a good current lie, I always forge   35
endorsements, as well as the bill.

ABSOLUTE

Well, take care you don't hurt your credit by offering
too much security. Is Mr Faulkland returned?

FAG

He is above, sir, changing his dress.

ABSOLUTE

Can you tell whether he has been informed of Sir   40
Anthony's and Miss Melville's arrival?

FAG

I fancy not, sir; he has seen no one since he came in but
his gentleman, who was with him at Bristol. I think, sir,
I hear Mr Faulkland coming down.

ABSOLUTE

Go tell him I am here.   45

FAG

Yes, sir. (*Going*) I beg pardon, sir, but should Sir Anthony
call, you will do me the favour to remember that we are
'*recruiting*', if you please.

ABSOLUTE

Well, well.

FAG

And in tenderness to my character, if your honour could   50
bring in the chairmen and waiters, I shall esteem it as an
obligation; for though I never scruple a lie to serve my
master, yet it *hurts* one's conscience, to be found out.   *Exit*

ABSOLUTE

Now for my whimsical friend. If he does not know that
his mistress is here, I'll tease him a little before I tell him.   55

Enter FAULKLAND

Faulkland, you're welcome to Bath again; you are
punctual in your return.

34–6   *whenever I . . . the bill* Fag compares his lie to a forged cheque endorsed with phoney
          signatures.
50   *in tenderness to my character* out of care for my public reputation
51   *chairmen* 76 (chairman 75)
52   *scruple a lie* hesitate to lie
54   *whimsical* capricious
55   *mistress* fiancée (Julia)

FAULKLAND

Yes; I had nothing to detain me, when I had finished the
business I went on. Well, what news since I left you?
How stand matters between you and Lydia? 60

ABSOLUTE

Faith, much as they were. I have not seen her since our
quarrel, however I expect to be recalled every hour.

FAULKLAND

Why don't you persuade her to go off with you at once?

ABSOLUTE

What, and lose two thirds of her fortune? You forget that,
my friend. No, no, I could have brought her to that long 65
ago.

FAULKLAND

Nay, then, you trifle too long. If you are sure of *her*,
propose to the aunt *in your own character*, and write to
Sir Anthony for his consent.

ABSOLUTE

Softly, softly; for though I am convinced my little Lydia 70
would elope with me as Ensign Beverley, yet am I by
no means certain that she would take me with the
impediment of our friends' consent, a regular humdrum
wedding, and the reversion of a good fortune on my side.
No, no, I must prepare her gradually for the discovery, 75
and make myself necessary to her before I risk it. Well,
but, Faulkland, you'll dine with us today at the hotel?

FAULKLAND

Indeed I cannot: I am not in spirits to be of such a party.

ABSOLUTE

By heavens! I shall forswear your company. You are the
most teasing, captious, incorrigible lover! Do love like 80
a man.

FAULKLAND

I own I am unfit for company.

68 *in your own character* as yourself
73 *friends'* ed. (friend's 75, 76)
74 *the reversion . . . my side* the inheritance (on his father's death) of a good fortune
82 *I own* I confess

ABSOLUTE

Am not *I* a lover; ay, and a romantic one too? Yet do I
carry everywhere with me such a confounded farrago of
doubts, fears, hopes, wishes, and all the flimsy furniture   85
of a country miss's brain?

FAULKLAND

Ah, Jack, your heart and soul are not, like mine, fixed
immutably on one only object. You throw for a large
stake, but, losing, you could stake and throw again: but I
have set my sum of happiness on this cast, and not to   90
succeed were to be stripped of all.

ABSOLUTE

But, for heaven's sake, what grounds for apprehension
can your whimsical brain conjure up at present?

FAULKLAND

What grounds for apprehension did you say? Heavens!
Are there not a thousand? I fear for her spirits, her health –   95
her life! My absence may fret her; her anxiety for my
return, her fears for me, may oppress her gentle temper.
And for her health, does not every hour bring me cause
to be alarmed? If it rains, some shower may even then
have chilled her delicate frame! If the wind be keen, some   100
rude blast may have affected her! The heat of noon,
the dews of the evening, may endanger the life of her
for whom only I value mine. O Jack, when delicate
and feeling souls are separated, there is not a feature in
the sky, not a movement of the elements, not an   105
aspiration of the breeze, but hints some cause for a lover's
apprehension!

ABSOLUTE

Ay, but we may choose whether we will take the hint or

---

84 *farrago* medley, hotchpotch
85 *flimsy furniture* paltry accoutrements
90 *cast* one throw of the dice (a gambling metaphor)
93 *at present?* (75 continues: Has Julia missed writing this last post? Or was her last too
tender, or too cool, or too grave, or too gay, or – FAULKLAND Nay, nay, Jack. ABSOLUTE
Why, her love, her honour, her prudence, you cannot doubt. FAULKLAND O! Upon my
soul I never have; but –)
106 *aspiration* breath

not. So then, Faulkland, if you were convinced that
Julia were well and in spirits, you would be entirely   110
content.

FAULKLAND

I should be happy beyond measure – I'm anxious only
for that.

ABSOLUTE

Then, to cure your anxiety at once, Miss Melville is in
perfect health, and is at this moment in Bath.   115

FAULKLAND

Nay, Jack, don't trifle with me.

ABSOLUTE

She is arrived here with my father within this hour.

FAULKLAND

Can you be serious?

ABSOLUTE

I thought you knew Sir Anthony better than to be
surprised at a sudden whim of this kind. Seriously then,   120
it is as I tell you upon my honour.

FAULKLAND

My dear friend! [*Calls*] Hollo! Du-Peigne! My hat! [*To* JACK]
My dear Jack! Now nothing on earth can give me a moment's
uneasiness.

Enter FAG

FAG

Sir, Mr Acres, just arrived, is below.   125

ABSOLUTE

Stay, Faulkland, this Acres lives within a mile of Sir
Anthony, and he shall tell you how your mistress has
been ever since you left her. Fag, show the gentleman up.

Exit FAG

FAULKLAND

What, is he much acquainted in the family?

109   *not. So* 76 (no. – well 75)
110   *were well* 76 (was well 75)
116   *trifle with* play with, dally with

ABSOLUTE

O, very intimate. I insist on your not going – besides, his   130
character will divert you.

FAULKLAND

Well, I should like to ask him a few questions.

ABSOLUTE

He is likewise a rival of mine – that is, of my *other self's* –
for he does not think his friend Captain Absolute ever saw
the lady in question; and it is ridiculous enough to   135
hear him complain to me of '*one Beverley*, a concealed
skulking rival, who –'

FAULKLAND

Hush! He's here.

Enter [BOB] ACRES

ACRES

Ha! My dear friend, noble Captain, and honest Jack, how
dost thou? Just arrived, faith, as you see. [*To* FAULKLAND]   140
Sir, your humble servant. [*To* ABSOLUTE] Warm work on
the roads, Jack. Od's whips and wheels, I've travelled
like a comet, with a tail of dust all the way as long
as the Mall.

ABSOLUTE

Ah, Bob, you are indeed an eccentric planet, but we   145
know your attraction hither. Give me leave to introduce
Mr Faulkland to you: Mr Faulkland, Mr Acres.

ACRES

[*To* FAULKLAND] Sir, I am most heartily glad to see you.
Sir, I solicit your connections. [*To* ABSOLUTE] Hey,
Jack! What, this is Mr Faulkland, who –   150

---

137 *skulking* sneaking or hiding
139 During this scene Acres often does not hear what Faulkland says. Acres may be in a world
     of his own – or slightly deaf; alternatively Faulkland may address himself exclusively to Jack.
142 *Od's whips and wheels* the first example of Acres' new form of swearing in which the
     oaths used relate to the subject spoken about
144 *the Mall* runs along the northern boundary of St James Park from Trafalgar Square to
     Buckingham House (as it then was)
145 *eccentric* both (of a person) odd or capricious in behaviour or appearance, and (of an
     orbit) not circular
146 *attraction* here meaning both 'attraction in love' and 'the magnetic attraction of a planet'
     (so continuing the astronomical metaphor)
149 *solicit your connections* hope to know you better

ABSOLUTE

Ay, Bob, Miss Melville's Mr Faulkland.

ACRES

Odso! She and your father can be but just arrived before
me. I suppose you have seen them. Ah! Mr Faulkland,
you are indeed a happy man.

FAULKLAND

I have not seen Miss Melville yet, sir. I hope she enjoyed   155
full health and spirits in Devonshire?

ACRES

Never knew her better in my life, sir, never better. Od's
blushes and blooms, she has been as healthy as the
German Spa.

FAULKLAND

Indeed! I did hear that she had been a little indisposed.   160

ACRES

False, false, sir; only said to vex you. Quite the reverse, I
assure you.

FAULKLAND

There, Jack, you see she has the advantage of me; I had
almost fretted myself ill.

ABSOLUTE

Now are you angry with your mistress for not having   165
been sick.

FAULKLAND

No, no, you misunderstand me. Yet surely a little trifling
indisposition is not an unnatural consequence of absence
from those we love. Now confess – isn't there something
unkind in this violent, robust, unfeeling health?   170

ABSOLUTE

O, it was very unkind of her to be well in your absence to
be sure!

ACRES

Good apartments, Jack.

FAULKLAND

Well, sir, but you were saying that Miss Melville has been

---

152 *Odso* from 'Godso' – a mild expletive
159 *German Spa* Spa was the name of a continental town (now in Belgium) famous for its
     mineral springs; all other 'spa' towns are so called because of it

so *exceedingly* well. What, then she has been merry and   175
gay I suppose? Always in spirits, hey?

ACRES

Merry? Od's crickets! She has been the belle and spirit of
the company wherever she has been. So lively and
entertaining! So full of wit and humour!

FAULKLAND

There, Jack, there. O, by my soul, there is an innate levity   180
in woman that nothing can overcome. What! Happy – and
I away?

ABSOLUTE

Have done. How foolish this is! Just now you were only
apprehensive for your mistress's *spirits*.

FAULKLAND

Why, Jack, have I been the joy and spirit of the company?   185

ABSOLUTE

No, indeed, you have not.

FAULKLAND

Have I been lively and entertaining?

ABSOLUTE

O, upon my word, I acquit you.

FAULKLAND

Have I been full of wit and humour?

ABSOLUTE

No, faith. To do you justice, you have been confoundedly   190
stupid indeed.

ACRES

What's the matter with the gentleman?

ABSOLUTE

He is only expressing his great satisfaction at hearing that
Julia has been so well and happy – that's all, hey, Faulkland?

FAULKLAND

O, I am rejoiced to hear it. Yes, yes, she has a *happy*   195
disposition!

---

177 *crickets* known for their chirping and so proverbially said to be 'merry'
     belle and spirit most beautiful and vivacious member
180 *innate levity* inborn lightness
188 *acquit* declare not guilty (a legal term)
190 *confoundedly* 76 (confounded 75)

ACRES

That she has indeed. Then she is so accomplished: so sweet
a voice; so expert at her harpsichord; such a mistress of
flat and sharp, squallante, rumblante, and quiverante!
There was this time month – Od's minims and crotchets! –   200
how she did chirrup at Mrs Piano's concert.

FAULKLAND

There again – what say you to this? You see she has been
all mirth and song; not a thought of me!

ABSOLUTE

Foh, man, is not music 'the food of love'?

FAULKLAND

Well, well, it may be so. Pray Mr – what's his damned   205
name? Do you remember what songs Miss Melville sung?

ACRES

Not I, indeed.

ABSOLUTE

Stay now, they were some pretty, melancholy, 'purling
stream' airs, I warrant. Perhaps you may recollect. Did
she sing 'When absent from my soul's delight'?   210

ACRES

No, that wa'n't it.

ABSOLUTE

Or 'Go, gentle gales!' (*Sings*) 'Go, gentle gales!'

199 *squallante, rumblante, and quiverante* made-up terms intended to sound French. As
     they come from the English 'squalling', 'rumbling' and 'quivering' they are not very
     complimentary.
200 *this time month* a month ago
     minims and crotchets 'half-notes' and 'quarter notes' in music
201 *Piano* the instrument of that name had only just been invented and was still known as
     the 'pianoforte'. The word 'piano' is here used in its musical (Italian) sense meaning 'quiet'.
204 *is not . . . love* From the opening of Shakespeare's *Twelfth Night* I.i.1: 'If music be the food
     of love, play on . . .'
208–9 *'purling stream' airs* gentle, sentimental songs – but the phrase pokes fun at their hack-
     neyed, clichéd nature
210 *'When absent . . . delight'* Song VI from *Twelve Songs Set to Music . . . Opera Quarta* by
     William Jackson (c. 1755), 14–19: 'When absent from my soul's delight, / What terrors fill
     my troubled breast / Once more returned to thy loved sight, / Hope too returns, my fears
     have rest . . . '
212 *'Go gentle gales'* Song V from Jackson's *Twelve Songs*, 10–14: 'Go, gentle gales; go, gentle
     gales; / And bear my sighs away . . . '

ACRES

O no! Nothing like it. Ods, now I recollect one of them. (*Sings*) 'My heart's my own, my will is free.'

FAULKLAND

Fool! Fool that I am to fix all my happiness on such a   215
trifler! 'Sdeath! To make herself the pipe and balladmonger of a circle! To soothe her light heart with catches and glees! What can you say to this, sir?

ABSOLUTE

Why, that I should be glad to hear my mistress had been so merry, *sir*.   220

FAULKLAND

Nay, nay, nay: I am not sorry that she has been happy – no, no, I am glad of that. I would not have had her sad or sick. Yet surely a sympathetic heart would have shown itself, even in the choice of a song. She might have been temperately healthy, and, somehow, plaintively gay – but   225
she has been dancing too, I doubt not!

ACRES

What does the gentleman say about dancing?

ABSOLUTE

He says the lady we speak of dances as well as she sings.

ACRES

Ay, truly, does she. There was at our last race-ball –

FAULKLAND

Hell and the devil! There! There! I told you so, I told you   230
so! O, she thrives in my absence! Dancing! But her whole feelings have been in opposition with mine! I have been anxious, silent, pensive, sedentary; my days have been hours of care, my nights of watchfulness. She has been all Health! Spirit! Laugh! Song! Dance! O, damned,   235
damned levity!

---

213   *Ods* 76 (Ods slips 75)
214   '*My heart's my own, my will is free*' from Isaac Bickerstaff's comic opera *Love in a Village* (1762), I.i: 'My heart's my own, my will is free, / And so shall be my voice; / No mortal man shall wed with me, / Till first he's made my choice.'
216   *pipe and balladmonger* singer and ballad-seller
217–18 *catches and glees* songs to be sung in rounds and unaccompanied part-songs
229   *race-ball* ball held after a day of horse-races

ABSOLUTE

For heaven's sake! Faulkland, don't expose yourself so. Suppose she has danced, what then? Does not the ceremony of society often oblige –

FAULKLAND

Well, well, I'll contain myself. Perhaps, as you say, for form sake. What, Mr Acres, you were praising Miss Melville's manner of dancing a *minuet*, hey?   240

ACRES

O I dare insure her for that, but what I was going to speak of was her *country-dancing*. Od's swimmings, she has such an air with her!   245

FAULKLAND

Now disappointment on her! Defend this, Absolute, why don't you defend this? Country-dances! Jigs and reels! Am I to blame now? A minuet I could have forgiven. I should not have minded that; I say I should not have regarded a minuet – but *country-dances*! Zounds! Had she   250
made one in a *cotillion*, I believe I could have forgiven even that. But to be monkey-led for a night! To run the gauntlet through a string of amorous palming puppies! To show paces like a managed *filly*! O Jack, there never can be but *one* man in the world, whom a truly modest   255
and delicate woman ought to pair with in a *country-dance*; and even then, the rest of the couples should be her great uncles and aunts!

---

237   *don't expose yourself so* don't lay yourself so open (to ridicule)
242   *minuet* stately, dignified, slow dance performed by two people
243   *insure her for that* vouch for her ability at that
244   *country-dancing* fast-paced, boisterous dances involving mingling and exchanging partners
        swimmings may imply smooth gliding movements as in water, or giddiness as when dizzy
251   *cotillion* elaborate French social dance, more lively than a minuet, but not as lively as a country-dance
252   *monkey-led* led or partnered by 'monkeys' (mischievous people, 'apes of fashion')
252–3   *run the gauntlet* a military punishment in which the victim runs between rows of men who strike at him.
253   *palming* (1) touching with the palm; (2) deceitful or capable of trickery
254   *managed filly* well-trained mare (a horse that has been taught the stepping and moving of the *manège*); so performing to the command of others – and showing off. Faulkland's metaphors show that he is becoming obsessed with the animal nature of the dance.
256   *delicate* fastidious

ABSOLUTE

Ay, to be sure! Grandfathers and grandmothers!

FAULKLAND

If there be but one vicious mind in the set, 'twill spread   260
like a contagion. The action of their pulse beats to the
lascivious movement of the jig; their quivering,
warmbreathed sighs impregnate the very air; the atmosphere
becomes electrical to love – and each amorous spark darts
through every link of the chain! I must leave you. I own I   265
am somewhat flurried, and that confounded looby has
perceived it.   *Going*

ABSOLUTE

Nay, but stay, Faulkland, and thank Mr Acres for his
good news.

FAULKLAND

Damn his news!   *Exit*   270

ABSOLUTE

Ha, ha, ha! Poor Faulkland! Five minutes since, 'nothing on
earth could give him a moment's uneasiness!'

ACRES

The gentleman wa'n't angry at my praising his mistress,
was he?

ABSOLUTE

A little jealous, I believe, Bob.   275

ACRES

You don't say so? Ha, ha! Jealous of me – that's a good
joke!

ABSOLUTE

There's nothing strange in that, Bob. Let me tell you, that
sprightly grace and insinuating manner of yours will do
some mischief among the girls here.   280

---

260 *set* the number required to perform a country-dance
263–4 *the atmosphere becomes electrical* the atmosphere is charged (drawing loving feelings
       from the dancers)
265 *chain* line of dancers
266 *looby* lout, country bumpkin
267 *perceived it* 76 (75 continues: ABSOLUTE Ay, ay, you are in a hurry to throw yourself at
       Julia's feet. FAULKLAND I'm not in a humour to be trifled with. I shall see her only to
       upbraid her. (*Going*))
271 *Five minutes since* Five minutes ago

ACRES

Ah, you joke – ha, ha! Mischief? Ha, ha! But you know I
am not my own property; my dear Lydia has forestalled
me. She could never abide me in the country because I
used to dress so badly, but – od's frogs and tambours – I
shan't take matters so here. Now Ancient Madam has no   285
voice in it. I'll make my old clothes know who's master.
I shall straightway cashier the hunting-frock and render my
leather breeches incapable. My hair has been in training
some time.

ABSOLUTE

Indeed!   290

ACRES

Ay, and tho'ff the side-curls are a little restive, my
hind-part takes to it very kindly.

ABSOLUTE

O, you'll polish, I doubt not.

ACRES

Absolutely – I propose so. Then, if I can find out this
Ensign Beverley, od's triggers and flints, I'll make him   295
know the difference o't.

ABSOLUTE

Spoke like a man. But pray, Bob, I observe you have got
an odd kind of a new method of swearing.

ACRES

Ha, ha! You've taken notice of it. 'Tis genteel, isn't it? I
didn't invent it myself, though; but a commander in our   300

282–3 *forestalled me* held me back (from pursuing other women)
  284 *frogs* ornamental braided loops that fitted over spindle-shaped buttons and were used
       to secure great coats
       tambours embroidery-frames (or pieces of embroidery)
  285 *Ancient Madam* Acres' mother
  287 *cashier* dismiss from service
  288 *incapable* unable to be worn
       in training Acres is growing his own hair but, as with his clothes, he describes his actions
       using military vocabulary
  291 *tho'ff* the same country dialect as is used by Thomas the coachman; it is greeted with a
       similar conversation on the need to 'polish'.
  295 *triggers and flints* a reference to duelling pistols (the trigger released the hammer which
       struck the flint, causing a spark that would ignite the gunpowder and fire the bullet)
  299 *genteel* gentlemanly, well-bred

militia – a great scholar, I assure you – says that there is
no meaning in the common oaths, and that nothing but
their antiquity makes them respectable, because, he says,
the ancients would never stick to an oath or two, but
would say 'By Jove!' or 'By Bacchus!' or 'By Mars!' or   305
'By Venus!' or 'By Pallas!' according to the sentiment.
So that to swear with propriety, says my little major, the
'oath should be an echo to the sense'; and this we call the
'oath referential', or 'sentimental swearing'. Ha, ha, ha!
'Tis genteel, isn't it?   310

ABSOLUTE

Very genteel, and very new indeed; and I dare say will
supplant all other figures of imprecation.

ACRES

Ay, ay; the best terms will grow obsolete. 'Damns' have
had their day.

Enter FAG

FAG

Sir, there is a gentleman below, desires to see you. Shall I   315
show him into the parlour?

ABSOLUTE

Ay, you may.

ACRES

Well, I must be gone.

ABSOLUTE

Stay – who is it, Fag?

FAG

Your father, sir.   320

ABSOLUTE

You puppy, why didn't you show him up directly?

Exit FAG

---

301   *militia* part-time soldiers made from the civilian population
305–6   *Jove . . . Pallas* Jove was the king of gods; Bacchus the god of wine; Mars the god of war;
          Venus the god of love; and Pallas the god of wisdom.
306   *according to the sentiment* according to the opinion or feelings expressed
308   *the 'oath should be an echo to the sense'* Corruption of Alexander Pope's ''Tis not enough
          no Harshness gives Offence, / The *Sound* must seem an *Eccho* to the *Sense*' from *An Essay
          in Criticism* (1711), 364–5.
309   *'sentimental swearing'* In a play that parodies the 'sentimental', the use of the term for a
          variety of swearing is, presumably, intentional.

ACRES

You have business with Sir Anthony. I expect a message
from Mrs Malaprop at my lodgings. I have sent also to my
dear friend Sir Lucius O'Trigger. Adieu, Jack. We must
meet at night when you shall give me a dozen bumpers to   325
little Lydia.

ABSOLUTE

That I will with all my heart.

Exit ACRES

ABSOLUTE

Now for a parental lecture. I hope he has heard nothing of
the business that has brought me here. I wish the gout
had held him fast in Devonshire, with all my soul!   330

Enter SIR ANTHONY [ABSOLUTE]

Sir, I am delighted to see you here, and looking so well!
Your sudden arrival at Bath made me apprehensive for
your health.

SIR ANTHONY

Very apprehensive, I dare say, Jack. What, you are
recruiting here, hey?   335

ABSOLUTE

Yes, sir, I am on duty.

SIR ANTHONY

Well, Jack, I am glad to see you, though I did not expect
it, for I was going to write to you on a little matter of
business. Jack, I have been considering that I grow old
and infirm, and shall probably not trouble you long.   340

ABSOLUTE

Pardon me, sir, I never saw you look more strong and
hearty; and I pray frequently that you may continue so.

SIR ANTHONY

I hope your prayers may be heard with all my heart. Well
then, Jack, I have been considering that I am so strong
and hearty, I may continue to plague you a long time.   345
Now, Jack, I am sensible that the income of your

---

325 *night* 76 (75 omits 'when' and has instead: od's bottles and glasses!)
     bumpers glasses filled to the brim i.e. toasts
346 *sensible* aware

commission, and what I have hitherto allowed you, is but a small pittance for a lad of your spirit.

ABSOLUTE

Sir, you are very good.

SIR ANTHONY

And it is my wish, while yet I live, to have my boy make   350
some figure in the world. I have resolved, therefore, to fix you at once in a noble independence.

ABSOLUTE

Sir, your kindness overpowers me. Such generosity makes the gratitude of reason more lively than the sensations even of filial affection.   355

SIR ANTHONY

I am glad you are so sensible of my attention; and you shall be master of a large estate in a few weeks.

ABSOLUTE

Let my future life, sir, speak my gratitude: I cannot express the sense I have of your munificence. Yet, sir, I presume you would not wish me to quit the army?   360

SIR ANTHONY

O, that shall be as your wife chooses.

ABSOLUTE

My wife, sir!

SIR ANTHONY

Ay, ay, settle that between you; settle that between you.

ABSOLUTE

A *wife*, sir, did you say?

SIR ANTHONY

Ay, a wife. Why – did not I mention her before?   365

ABSOLUTE

Not a word of her, sir.

SIR ANTHONY

Odso! I mustn't forget *her* though. Yes, Jack, the

346–7   *income of your commission* army pay

348   *small pittance* A Captain in the army would receive about £190 a year; that, added to the £50 a year that Absolute's father gives him (see III.i.15) will scarcely have provided the funds to live as a gentleman.

350–1   *make some figure* make a significant impression

356   *sensible of my attention* conscious of my consideration

366   *her* 76 (it 75)

independence I was talking of is by a marriage. The
fortune is saddled with a wife – but I suppose that makes
no difference?   370

ABSOLUTE

Sir! Sir! You amaze me!

SIR ANTHONY

Why, what the devil's the matter with the fool? Just now
you were all gratitude and duty.

ABSOLUTE

I was, sir: you talked to me of independence and a fortune,
but not a word of a wife.   375

SIR ANTHONY

Why what difference does that make? Od's life, sir! If you
have the estate, you must take it with the livestock on it,
as it stands.

ABSOLUTE

If my happiness is to be the price, I must beg leave to
decline the purchase. Pray, sir, who is the lady?   380

SIR ANTHONY

What's that to you, sir? Come, give me your promise to
love and to marry her directly.

ABSOLUTE

Sure, sir, this is not very reasonable, to summon my
affections for a lady I know nothing of!

SIR ANTHONY

I am sure, sir, 'tis more unreasonable in you to *object* to   385
a lady you know nothing of.

ABSOLUTE

Then, sir, I must tell you plainly, that my inclinations are
fixed on another. Sir, my heart is engaged to an angel.

SIR ANTHONY

Then pray let it send an excuse. It is very sorry but
business prevents its waiting on her.   390

ABSOLUTE

But my vows are pledged to her.

---

377   *livestock* cattle and other animals on an estate
388   *another.* 76 (75 continues: SIR ANTHONY They are, are they? Well, that's lucky – because
     you will have more merit in your obedience to me.
390   *business* other engagements, serious matters or financial affairs

SIR ANTHONY

Let her foreclose, Jack; let her foreclose. They are not
worth redeeming. Besides, you have the angel's vows in
exchange, I suppose; so there can be no loss there.

ABSOLUTE

You must excuse me, sir, if I tell you, once for all, that in   395
this point I cannot obey you.

SIR ANTHONY

Hark'ee Jack. I have heard you for some time with
patience. I have been cool, quite cool; but take care. You
know I am compliance itself when I am not thwarted; no
one more easily led when I have my own way – but don't   400
put me in a frenzy!

ABSOLUTE

Sir, I must repeat it: in this, I cannot obey you!

SIR ANTHONY

Now, damn me, if ever I call you *Jack* again while I live!

ABSOLUTE

Nay, sir, but hear me.

SIR ANTHONY

Sir, I won't hear a word – not a word! Not one word! So   405
give me your promise by a nod, and I'll tell you what,
Jack – I mean, you dog – if you don't, by –

ABSOLUTE

What, sir, promise to link myself to some mass of
ugliness! To –

SIR ANTHONY

Zounds, sirrah, the lady shall be as ugly as I choose. She   410
shall have a hump on each shoulder; she shall be as
crooked as the Crescent; her one eye shall roll like the

392–3 *not worth redeeming* Sir Anthony picks up on the potential financial implication of
Absolute's word 'pledged'. According to Sir Anthony, Absolute gave the 'angel' vows as
security for continued love. But if he fails to repay and she, like a money-lender, then
'forecloses' (ends the agreement and takes possession of the security), no loss will be
incurred as the transaction consisted only of words. Besides, as the 'angel' also made
vows, Absolute will still have profited for what he gave.

410   *sirrah* alteration of 'sir' used to imply inferiority in the person so addressed.

412   *the Crescent* the Royal Crescent, a crescent-shaped street in Bath, begun in 1767 by the
architect John Wood the Younger

412–13 *the bull's in Cox's museum* James Cox had an exhibition of mechanical toys, curiosities
and automatons that he showed in Spring Gardens, London, between 1772 and 1775.

bull's in Cox's museum; she shall have a skin like a
mummy; and the beard of a Jew: she shall be all this,
sirrah! Yet I'll make you ogle her all day, and sit up all   415
night to write sonnets on her beauty.

ABSOLUTE

This is reason and moderation indeed!

SIR ANTHONY

None of your sneering, puppy! No grinning, jackanapes!

ABSOLUTE

Indeed, sir, I never was in a worse humour for mirth in
my life.   420

SIR ANTHONY

'Tis false, sir! I know you are laughing in your sleeve:
I know you'll grin when I am gone, sirrah!

ABSOLUTE

Sir, I hope I know my duty better.

SIR ANTHONY

None of your passion, sir! None of your violence, if you
please. It won't do with me, I promise you.   425

ABSOLUTE

Indeed, sir, I never was cooler in my life.

SIR ANTHONY

'Tis a confounded lie! I know you are in a passion in your
heart; I know you are, you hypocritical young dog! But it
won't do.

ABSOLUTE

Nay, sir, upon my word.   430

SIR ANTHONY

So you will fly out! Can't you be cool, like me? What the
devil good can *passion* do? *Passion* is of no service, you
impudent, insolent, over-bearing reprobate! There you
sneer again! Don't provoke me! But you rely upon the
mildness of my temper – you do, you dog! You play upon   435
the meekness of my disposition! Yet take care. The
patience of a saint may be overcome at last! But mark!

---

414 *mummy* embalmed dead body
418 *jackanapes* ape, monkey, impertinent youngster. Sir Anthony starts to say 'Jack' again,
     realises he has determined not to use the name, and turns the word into this insult.
431 *fly out* lash out in anger
436 *meekness* 76 (weakness 75)

I give you six hours and a half to consider of this. If you
then agree, without any condition, to do everything on
earth that I choose, why, confound you, I may in time   440
forgive you. If not, zounds, don't enter the same
hemisphere with me; don't dare to breathe the same air, or
use the same light with me; but get an atmosphere and a
sun of your own! I'll strip you of your commission; I'll
lodge a five-and-three-pence in the hands of trustees, and   445
you shall live on the interest. I'll disown you, I'll
disinherit you, I'll unget you! And damn me, if ever I call
you Jack again!   *Exit*

ABSOLUTE

Mild, gentle, considerate father, I kiss your hands. What a
tender method of giving his opinion in these matters Sir   450
Anthony has! I dare not trust him with the truth. I wonder
what old, wealthy hag it is that he wants to bestow on me!
Yet he married himself for love, and was in his youth a
bold intriguer, and a gay companion!

Enter FAG

FAG

Assuredly, sir, our father is wrath to a degree. He comes   455
down stairs eight or ten steps at a time muttering,
growling, and thumping the banisters all the way. I, and
the cook's dog, stand bowing at the door. Rap! He gives me
a stroke on the head with his cane; bids me carry that to
my master, then, kicking the poor turnspit into the area,   460
damns us all for a puppy triumvirate! Upon my credit,
sir, were I in your place, and found my father such very
bad company, I should certainly drop his acquaintance.

443–4   *a sun* 76 (sun 75)
 444   *strip you of your commission* reduce you to the ranks
 445   *lodge . . . trustees* Sir Anthony threatens to cut Jack's inheritance to a quarter of a guinea
 447   *unget* unbeget, unconceive
 448   s.d. (om. s.d. *Absolute solus* 75, 76)
 454   *intriguer* lover, seducer
458–9   *gives me a stroke* hits me
 460   *turnspit* a dog whose job is to turn a roasting spit by walking in a treadmill
        area steps to the basement at the front of a house
 461   *triumvirate* three men ruling jointly – in this instance, Jack, Fag and the cook's dog

ABSOLUTE

Cease your impertinence, sir, at present. Did you come in
for nothing more? Stand out of the way!   465

Pushes [FAG] *aside, and exit*[*s*]

FAG

So! Sir Anthony trims my master. He is afraid to reply to
his father, then vents his spleen on poor Fag! When one is
vexed by one person, to revenge one's self on another, who
happens to come in the way is the vilest injustice! Ah, it
shows the worst temper; the basest –   470

Enter ERRAND-BOY

ERRAND-BOY

Mr Fag! Mr Fag! Your master calls you.

FAG

Well, you little, dirty puppy, you need not bawl so! The
meanest disposition! The –

ERRAND-BOY

Quick, quick, Mr Fag.

FAG

'*Quick, quick*', you impudent jackanapes! Am I to be   475
commanded by you too? You little, impertinent,
insolent, kitchen-bred –

Exit, kicking and beating [ERRAND BOY]

---

465   s.d. ed. (*pushes him aside, and Exit* 75, 76); (om. s.d. *Fag solus* 75, 76)
466   *trims* reproves, scolds
467   *vents his spleen* unleashes his anger
477   s.d. ed. (*Exit, kicking . . . him* 75, 76)

[Act II,] Scene ii

The North Parade

Enter LUCY

LUCY

So. I shall have another rival to add to my mistress's list:
Captain Absolute. However, I shall not enter his name till
my purse has received notice in form. Poor Acres is
dismissed! Well, I have done him a last friendly office in
letting him know that Beverley was here before him. Sir   5
Lucius is generally more punctual, when he expects to
hear from his '*dear Dalia*', as he calls her. I wonder he's
not here! I have a little scruple of conscience from this
deceit; though I should not be paid so well if my hero
knew that *Delia* was near fifty, and her own mistress.   10

Enter SIR LUCIUS O'TRIGGER

SIR LUCIUS

Hah! My little embassadress! Upon my conscience I have
been looking for you; I have been on the South Parade
this half-hour.

LUCY

(*Speaking simply*) O gemini! And I have been waiting for
your worship here on the North.   15

SIR LUCIUS

Faith! Maybe that was the reason we did not meet; and it
is very comical too, how you could go out and I not see
you, for I was only taking a nap at the Parade coffee-house,
and I chose the *window* on purpose that I might not miss you.

LUCY

My stars! Now I'd wager a sixpence I went by while you   20
were asleep.

3 *notice in form* formal notice, i.e. a bribe
4 *office* job
7 The spelling reflects Lucius' Irish pronunciation.
10 *mistress* 76 (75 continues: I could not have thought he would have been so nice, when
    there's a golden egg in the case, as to care whether he has it from a pullet or an old hen!)
14 s.d. *simply* foolishly
18 *Parade coffee-house* 'Mr. Pritchard's [coffee-house] fronts the North-Parade, and is there-
    fore called the Parade Coffee-House', *New Bath Guide*, 1771, 33

SIR LUCIUS

Sure enough it must have been so. And I never dreamt it
was so late, till I waked. Well, but, my little girl, have you
got nothing for me?

LUCY

Yes, but I have: I've got a letter for you in my pocket.   25

SIR LUCIUS

O faith! I guessed you weren't come empty-handed. Well,
let me see what the dear creature says.

LUCY

There, Sir Lucius.   (*Gives him a letter*)

SIR LUCIUS

(*Reads*) 'Sir, there is often a sudden incentive impulse
in love, that has a greater induction than years of   30
domestic combination. Such was the commotion I felt at
the first superfluous view of Sir Lucius O'Trigger.' Very
pretty, upon my word. 'Female punctuation forbids me
to say more; yet let me add, that it will give me joy infallible
to find Sir Lucius worthy the last criterion of my   35
affections. Delia.' Upon my conscience, Lucy, your lady is
a great mistress of language. Faith, she's quite the queen
of the dictionary, for the devil a word dare refuse coming
at her call though one would think it was quite out of
hearing.   40

LUCY

Ay, sir, a lady of her experience.

SIR LUCIUS

Experience! What, at seventeen?

---

29 *incentive* provocative (not a malapropism); or, for, instinctive
30 *induction* an introductory process; or, for, inducement
31 *combination* being together
    commotion (presumably) for, emotion
32 *superfluous* for, superficial
33 *word* 76 (75 continues: 'As my motive is interested, you may be assured my love shall
    never be miscellaneous'. Very well.)
    punctuation for, punctilio, punctiliousness (good manners), compunction or, perhaps,
    unction
34 *infallible* (presumably) for, ineffable
35 *criterion* mark or trait, not a malapropism
36 *affections* 76 (75 continues: yours while meretricious)

LUCY

O true, sir, but then she reads so. My stars, how she will
read off-hand!

SIR LUCIUS

Faith, she must be very deep read to write this way, though   45
she is rather an arbitrary writer too, for here are a great
many poor words pressed into the service of this note, that
would get their *habeas corpus* from any court in
Christendom.

LUCY

Ah! Sir Lucius, if you were to hear how she talks of you!   50

SIR LUCIUS

O, tell her I'll make her the best husband in the world, and
Lady O'Trigger into the bargain! But we must get the old
gentlewoman's consent and do everything fairly.

LUCY

Nay, Sir Lucius, I thought you wa'n't rich enough to
be so nice!   55

SIR LUCIUS

Upon my word, young woman, you have hit it. I am so
poor that I can't afford to do a dirty action. If I did not
want money I'd steal your mistress and her fortune with
a great deal of pleasure. However, my pretty girl (*Gives
her money*), here's a little something to buy you a ribbon;   60
and meet me in the evening, and I'll give you an answer
to this. So, hussy, take a kiss beforehand, to put you in
mind. (*Kisses* [LUCY])

LUCY

O lud, Sir Lucius, I never seed such a gemman! My lady
won't like you if you're so impudent.   65

---

44   *off-hand* straight off
47   *pressed* forcibly enlisted (men were sometimes forced by a 'press-gang' into the armed
services)
48   *habeas corpus* literally 'you may have the body'; the opening words of a writ to prevent
a person being imprisoned without charge – hence, 'release'
49   *Christendom* 76. (75 continues: However, when affection guides the pen, Lucy, he must
be a brute who finds fault with the style.)
55   *nice* fastidious, scrupulous
60   *ribbon* ed. (ribband 75, 76)
63   *Kisses* LUCY ed. (*Kisses her* 75, 76)
64   *seed such a gemman* saw such a gentleman – in Lucy's carefully 'simplistic' language

SIR LUCIUS

Faith she will, Lucy. That same – foh, what's the name of it? – '*modesty*!' is a quality in a lover more praised by the women than liked. So, if your mistress asks you whether Sir Lucius ever gave you a kiss, tell her *fifty*, my dear.

LUCY

What, would you have me tell her a lie?   70

SIR LUCIUS

Ah, then, you baggage, I'll make it a truth presently.

LUCY

For shame now! Here is someone coming.

SIR LUCIUS

O faith, I'll quiet your conscience!

Sees FAG. *Exit, humming a tune*

Enter FAG

FAG

So, so, ma'am. I humbly beg pardon.

LUCY

O lud! Now, Mr Fag, you flurry one so.   75

FAG

Come, come, Lucy, here's no one by, so a little less simplicity, with a grain or two more sincerity, if you please. You play false with us, madam. I saw you give the baronet a letter. My master shall know this, and if he don't call him out, I will.   80

LUCY

Ha, ha, ha! You gentlemen's gentlemen are so hasty. That letter was from Mrs Malaprop, simpleton. She is taken with Sir Lucius's address.

FAG

How! What tastes some people have! Why I suppose I have walked by her window an hundred times. But what   85 says our young lady? Any message to my master?

71 *baggage* saucy girl, impudent thing
80 *call him out* challenge him to a duel
83 *address* manners
84 *How!* 76 (om. 75)

LUCY

Sad news, Mr Fag! A worse rival than Acres! Sir
Anthony Absolute has proposed his son.

FAG

What, Captain Absolute?

LUCY

Even so. I overheard it all.   90

FAG

Ha, ha, ha! Very good, faith. Goodbye, Lucy, I must
away with this news.

LUCY

Well, you may laugh, but it is true, I assure you. (*Going*) But,
Mr Fag, tell your master not to be cast down by this.

FAG

O, he'll be so disconsolate!   95

LUCY

And charge him not to think of quarrelling with young
Absolute.

FAG

Never fear! Never fear!

LUCY

Be sure bid him keep up his spirits.

FAG

We will, we will.   100

Exeunt severally

Act III, Scene i

The North Parade

Enter [JACK] ABSOLUTE

ABSOLUTE

'Tis just as Fag told me, indeed. Whimsical enough, faith!
My father wants to *force* me to marry the very girl I am
plotting to run away with! He must not know of my
connection with her yet awhile. He has too summary a

4 *summary* hasty

method of proceeding in these matters. However, I'll read   5
my recantation instantly. My conversion is something
sudden, indeed, but I can assure him it is very *sincere*. So,
so, here he comes. He looks plaguy gruff.   *Steps aside*

Enter SIR ANTHONY [ABSOLUTE]

SIR ANTHONY

No, I'll die sooner than forgive him. *Die*, did I say? I'll
live these fifty years to plague him. At our last meeting,   10
his impudence had almost put me out of temper. An
obstinate, passionate, self-willed boy! Who can he take
after? This is my return for getting him before all his
brothers and sisters! For putting him, at twelve years old,
into a marching regiment, and allowing him fifty pounds   15
a year, beside his pay, ever since! But I have done with
him; he's anybody's son for me. I never will see him
more – never, never, never, never!

ABSOLUTE

[*Aside*] Now for a penitential face.

SIR ANTHONY

Fellow, get out of my way.   20

ABSOLUTE

Sir, you see a penitent before you.

SIR ANTHONY

I see an impudent scoundrel before me.

ABSOLUTE

A sincere penitent. I am come, sir, to acknowledge my
error, and to submit entirely to your will.

SIR ANTHONY

What's that?   25

---

5 *matters* (75 continues: and Lydia shall not yet lose her hopes of an elopement)
8 *plaguy* (here) extremely
13 *getting* begetting
14 *twelve years old* military commissions could be bought for children who thus attained
    early seniority
15 *marching regiment* regiment without settled quarters – so liable to be sent anywhere
18 *never . . . never* echoes the words of Shakespeare's *King Lear* over his dead daughter
    Cordelia, V.iii.307–8: 'Thou'lt come no more: / Never, never, never, never, never'. Both
    Lear and Absolute are stubbornly irrational, and both consider themselves fathers of
    ungrateful children – but to contrast the 'tragedy' of the two is absurd.
21 *penitent* repentant sinner

ABSOLUTE

I have been revolving, and reflecting, and considering on your past goodness, and kindness, and condescension to me.

SIR ANTHONY

Well, sir?

ABSOLUTE

I have been likewise weighing and balancing what you were pleased to mention concerning duty, and obedience, and authority.   30

SIR ANTHONY

Well, puppy?

ABSOLUTE

Why then, sir, the result of my reflections is a resolution to sacrifice every inclination of my own to your satisfaction.   35

SIR ANTHONY

Why now, you talk sense, absolute sense. I never heard anything more sensible in my life. Confound you; you shall be *Jack* again.

ABSOLUTE

I am happy in the appellation.

SIR ANTHONY

Why, then, Jack, my dear Jack, I will now inform you   40
who the lady really is. Nothing but your passion and violence, you silly fellow, prevented my telling you at first. Prepare, Jack, for wonder and rapture: prepare. What think you of Miss Lydia Languish?

ABSOLUTE

Languish! What, the Languishes of Worcestershire?   45

SIR ANTHONY

Worcestershire! No. Did you never meet Mrs Malaprop and her niece, Miss Languish, who came into our country just before you were last ordered to your regiment?

ABSOLUTE

Malaprop! Languish! I don't remember ever to have heard the names before. Yet, stay – I think I do recollect   50

27 *condescension* kindness to an inferior
36 *absolute sense* Sir Anthony draws attention to their surname
47 *country* neighbourhood

something. *Languish*! *Languish*! She squints, don't she?
A little, red-haired girl?

SIR ANTHONY
Squints? A red-haired girl! Zounds, no.

ABSOLUTE
Then I must have forgot; it can't be the same person.

SIR ANTHONY
Jack! Jack! What think you of blooming, love-breathing   55
seventeen?

ABSOLUTE
As to that, sir, I am quite indifferent. If I can please you
in the matter, 'tis all I desire.

SIR ANTHONY
Nay, but Jack, such eyes! Such eyes! So innocently wild!
So bashfully irresolute! Not a glance but speaks and   60
kindles some thought of love! Then, Jack, her cheeks! Her
cheeks, Jack! So deeply blushing at the insinuations of her
tell-tale eyes! Then, Jack, her lips! O Jack, lips smiling at
their own discretion; and if not smiling, more sweetly
pouting; more lovely in sullenness!   65

ABSOLUTE
[*Aside*] That's she indeed. Well done, old gentleman!

SIR ANTHONY
Then, Jack, her neck. O Jack! Jack!

ABSOLUTE
And which is to be mine, sir, the niece or the aunt?

SIR ANTHONY
Why, you unfeeling, insensible puppy, I despise you.
When I was of your age, such a description would have   70
made me fly like a rocket! The *aunt*, indeed! Od's life!
When I ran away with your mother, I would not have
touched anything old or ugly to gain an empire.

ABSOLUTE
Not to please your father, sir?

SIR ANTHONY
To please my father! Zounds! Not to please – O, my father!   75
Odso! Yes, yes! If my father indeed had desired – that's

---

67 *neck* everything exposed by women's fashionable dress of the period – neck, shoulders
and the upper parts of the breasts
71 *rocket* firework

quite another matter. Though he wa'n't the indulgent father that I am, Jack.

ABSOLUTE

I dare say not, sir.

SIR ANTHONY

But, Jack, you are not sorry to find your mistress is so 80 beautiful.

ABSOLUTE

Sir, I repeat it; if I please you in this affair, 'tis all I desire. Not that I think a woman the worse for being handsome; but, sir, if you please to recollect, you before hinted something about a hump or two, one eye, and a few more 85 graces of that kind. Now, without being very nice, I own I should rather choose a wife of mine to have the usual number of limbs, and a limited quantity of back: and though *one* eye may be very agreeable, yet as the prejudice has always run in favour of *two*, I would not 90 wish to affect a singularity in that article.

SIR ANTHONY

What a phlegmatic sot it is! Why, sirrah, you're an anchorite! A vile insensible stock! You, a soldier! You're a walking block, fit only to dust the company's regimentals on! Od's life! I've a great mind to marry 95 the girl myself!

ABSOLUTE

I am entirely at your disposal, sir; if you should think of addressing Miss Languish yourself, I suppose you would have me marry the *aunt*; or if you should change your mind and take the old lady – 'tis the same to me – I'll 100 marry the *niece*.

SIR ANTHONY

Upon my word, Jack, thou'rt either a very great hypocrite, or – but, come, I know your indifference on such a subject must be all a lie. I'm sure it must. Come, now. Damn your

91 *affect a singularity* be 'singular' odd, or chose the 'single' (one)
92 *phlegmatic sot* dull fool
93 *anchorite* hermit
     stock block of wood
94 *block* wooden tailor's dummy on which army uniforms were placed so that they could be beaten free of dust; blockhead
99 *your* 76 (you're 75)

demure face! Come, confess, Jack: you have been lying   105
ha'n't you? You have been playing the hypocrite, hey! I'll
never forgive you, if you ha'n't been lying and playing the
hypocrite.

ABSOLUTE

I'm sorry, sir, that the respect and duty which I bear to
you should be so mistaken.   110

SIR ANTHONY

Hang your respect and duty! But – come along with me –
I'll write a note to Mrs Malaprop, and you shall visit the
lady directly. Her eyes shall be the Promethean torch to
you. Come along! I'll never forgive you if you don't come
back stark mad with rapture and impatience; if you don't,   115
egad, I'll marry the girl myself!

Exeunt

[Act III,] Scene ii

JULIA [MELVILLE]*'s dressing-room*

FAULKLAND [*alone*]

FAULKLAND

They told me Julia would return directly; I wonder she is
not yet come! How mean does this captious, unsatisfied
temper of mine appear to my cooler judgment! Yet I know
not that I indulge it in any other point; but on this one
subject, and to this one subject, whom I think I love   5

---

106 *ha'n't you?* 76 (75 continues: You have been lying, hey? I'll never forgive you if you ha'n't.
So now, own, my dear Jack,)

113 *directly.* 76 (75 continues: ABSOLUTE Where does she lodge, sir? SIR ANTHONY What a dull
question! Only on the Grove here. ABSOLUTE O, then I can call on her in my way to the
coffee-house. SIR ANTHONY In your way to the coffee-house! You'll set your heart down
in your way to the coffee-house, hey? Ah! You leaden-nerved, wooden-hearted dolt! But,
come along, you shall see her directly;)
Promethean torch In Greek mythology, Prometheus stole fire from the gods and gave it
to man.

116 *egad* a corruption of 'by God' – mild expletive

0 s.d. 1 ed. (*Faulkland solus* 75, 76)

5 *subject, whom* 76 (object, whom 75)

beyond my life, I am ever ungenerously fretful, and madly capricious! I am conscious of it, yet I cannot correct myself! What tender, honest joy sparkled in her eyes when we met! How delicate was the warmth of her expressions! I was ashamed to appear less happy, though   10
I had come resolved to wear a face of coolness and upbraiding. Sir Anthony's presence prevented my proposed expostulations: yet I must be satisfied that she has not been so *very* happy in my absence. She is coming! Yes! I know the nimbleness of her tread, when she thinks her   15
impatient Faulkland counts the moments of her stay.

Enter JULIA [MELVILLE]

JULIA

I had not hoped to see you again so soon.

FAULKLAND

Could I, Julia, be contented with my first welcome, restrained as we were by the presence of a third person?

JULIA

O Faulkland, when your kindness can make me thus   20
happy, let me not think that I discovered something of coldness in your first salutation.

FAULKLAND

'Twas but your fancy, Julia. I *was* rejoiced to see you – to see you in such health. Sure I had no cause for coldness?

JULIA

Nay, then, I see you have taken something ill. You must   25
not conceal from me what it is.

FAULKLAND

Well, then, shall I own to you that my joy at hearing of your health and arrival here, by your neighbour Acres, was somewhat damped by his dwelling much on the high spirits you had enjoyed in Devonshire – on your mirth,   30
your singing, dancing, and I know not what! For such is my temper, Julia, that I should regard every mirthful

---

7 *capricious* subject to sudden changes of feelings and emotions
21–2 *something of coldness* 76 (more coolness 75)
22 *salutation* 76 (75 continues: than my long-hoarded joy could have presaged.)
27 *to you* 76 (75 continues: but you will despise me, Julia. Nay, I despise myself for it. Yet I *will* own,)
29 *somewhat* 76 (something 75)

moment in your absence as a treason to constancy. The
mutual tear that steals down the cheek of parting lovers is
a compact that no smile shall live there till they meet again.   35

JULIA

Must I never cease to tax my Faulkland with this teasing
minute caprice? Can the idle reports of a silly boor weigh
in your breast against my tried affection?

FAULKLAND

They have no weight with me, Julia. No, no: I am happy if
you have been so – yet only say that you did not sing with   40
mirth, say that you *thought* of Faulkland in the dance.

JULIA

I never can be happy in your absence. If I wear a
countenance of content, it is to show that my mind holds
no doubt of my Faulkland's truth. If I seemed sad, it were
to make malice triumph, and say that I had fixed my heart   45
on one who left me to lament his roving, and my own
credulity. Believe me, Faulkland, I mean not to upbraid
you, when I say that I have often dressed sorrow in smiles,
lest my friends should guess whose unkindness had caused
my tears.   50

FAULKLAND

You were ever all goodness to me. O, I am a brute, when I
but admit a doubt of your true constancy!

JULIA

If ever, without such cause from you as I will not suppose
possible, you find my affections veering but a point, may I
become a proverbial scoff for levity, and base ingratitude.   55

FAULKLAND

Ah, Julia, that *last* word is grating to me. I would I had no
title to your *gratitude*! Search your heart, Julia; perhaps
what you have mistaken for love is but the warm effusion
of a too thankful heart!

36   *tax . . . with* accuse . . . of
38   *tried* proved
43   *countenance* face, appearance
46   *roving* wondering, infidelity
54   *veering but a point* changing direction minutely; a 'point' is one of the 32 points
      (divisions) on a mariner's compass
57   *title* claim

JULIA

For what quality must I love you?   60

FAULKLAND

For no quality! To regard me for any quality of mind or
understanding were only to *esteem* me. And, for person, I
have often wished myself deformed, to be convinced that
I owed no obligation *there* for any part of your affection.

JULIA

Where nature has bestowed a show of nice attention in the   65
features of a man, he should laugh at it as misplaced. I
have seen men who, in *this* vain article perhaps, might
rank above you; but my heart has never asked my eyes if it
were so or not.

FAULKLAND

Now this is not well from *you,* Julia. I despise person in a   70
man. Yet, if you loved me as I wish, though I were an
Ethiop, you'd think none so fair.

JULIA

I see you are determined to be unkind. The *contract* which
my poor father bound us in gives you more than a lover's
privilege.   75

FAULKLAND

Again, Julia, you raise ideas that feed and justify my
doubts. I would not have been more free. No, I am proud
of my restraint. Yet – yet – perhaps your high respect
alone for this solemn compact has fettered your
inclinations, which else had made a worthier choice. How   80
shall I be sure, had you remained unbound in thought and
promise, that I should still have been the object of your
persevering love?

JULIA

Then try me now. Let us be free as strangers as to what is

---

62 *person* appearance
67 *this vain article* this trivial matter (of personal appearance)
71–2 *an Ethiop* poetic term for an Ethiopian; often used in poetry of the time, as here, in
contrast with 'fair'
73 *contract* formal engagement
77–8 *I am proud of my restraint* 'I am proud of the fact that I am constrained' (by a marriage
contract)
79 *fettered* chained, manacled
80 *a worthier* 76 (worthier 75)

past: *my* heart will not feel more liberty!   85

FAULKLAND

There now! So hasty, Julia! So anxious to be free! If your
love for me were fixed and ardent, you would not loose
your hold, even though I wished it!

JULIA

O, you torture me to the heart! I cannot bear it.

FAULKLAND

I do not mean to distress you. If I loved you less, I should   90
never give you an uneasy moment. But hear me. All my
fretful doubts arise from this: women are not used to
weigh and separate the motives of their affections. The
cold dictates of prudence, gratitude, or filial duty may
sometimes be mistaken for the pleadings of the heart. I   95
would not boast – yet let me say that I have neither age,
person, or character to found dislike on; my fortune such
as few ladies could be charged with *indiscretion* in the
match. O Julia! When *love* receives such countenance
from *prudence*, nice minds will be suspicious of its *birth*.   100

JULIA

I know not whither your insinuations would tend. But as
they seem pressing to insult me, I will spare you the
regret of having done so. I have given you no cause for
this!   *Exit in tears*

FAULKLAND

In tears! Stay, Julia – stay but for a moment. The door is   105
fastened! Julia! My soul! But for one moment! I hear her
sobbing – 'sdeath, what a brute am I to use her thus! Yet
stay. Ay, she is coming now. How little resolution there is
in woman! How a few soft words can turn them! No,
faith, she is *not* coming either. Why, Julia, my love, say   110
but that you forgive me – come but to tell me that. Now,
this is being *too* resentful. Stay! She *is* coming too; I
thought she would: no *steadiness* in anything! Her going

99–100 *When love . . . birth* When 'love' is so supported by 'prudence', a careful mind will ques-
        tion how genuine is the love's origin
101   *But* 76 (om. 75)
107   *'sdeath* God's death

away must have been a mere trick then. She shan't see
that I was hurt by it. I'll affect indifference. (*Hums a tune,*   115
then listens) No, zounds, she's *not* coming! Nor don't
intend it, I suppose. This is not *steadiness*, but *obstinacy*!
Yet I deserve it. What, after so long an absence, to quarrel
with her tenderness! 'Twas barbarous and unmanly! I
should be ashamed to see her now. I'll wait till her just   120
resentment is abated, and when I distress her so again, may
I lose her for ever, and be linked instead to some antique
virago, whose gnawing passions and long-hoarded spleen
shall make me curse my folly half the day and all the night!

Exit

[Act III,] Scene iii

MRS MALAPROP's *lodgings*

MRS MALAPROP, *with a letter in her hand, and* [JACK]
ABSOLUTE

MRS MALAPROP
Your being Sir Anthony's son, Captain, would itself be a
sufficient accommodation; but from the ingenuity of your
appearance, I am convinced you deserve the character
here given of you.

ABSOLUTE
Permit me to say, madam, that as I never yet have had the   5
pleasure of seeing Miss Languish, my principal inducement
in this affair at present is the honour of being allied to
Mrs Malaprop, of whose intellectual accomplishments,
elegant manners, and unaffected learning, no tongue
is silent.   10

122–3 *antique virago* overbearing old woman

  0 s.d. 2 *with . . . hand* 76 (om. 75)
  2 *accommodation* for, recommendation
     ingenuity for, ingenuousness (openness)
  3 *character* (good) character reference

MRS MALAPROP

Sir, you do me infinite honour! I beg, Captain, you'll be seated. ([*They*] sit) Ah, few gentlemen, nowadays, know how to value the ineffectual qualities in a woman! Few think how a little knowledge becomes a gentlewoman! Men have no sense now but for the worthless flower of beauty!   15

ABSOLUTE

It is but too true indeed, ma'am. Yet I fear our ladies should share the blame: they think our admiration of *beauty* so great, that *knowledge* in *them* would be superfluous. Thus, like garden-trees, they seldom show fruit, till time has robbed them of the more specious blossom. Few, like Mrs   20
Malaprop and the orange-tree, are rich in both at once!

MRS MALAPROP

Sir, you overpower me with good-breeding. [*Aside*] He is the very pineapple of politeness! [*To* ABSOLUTE] You are not ignorant, Captain, that this giddy girl has somehow contrived to fix her affections on a beggarly,   25
strolling, eavesdropping Ensign, whom none of us have seen, and nobody knows anything of.

ABSOLUTE

O, I have heard the silly affair before. I'm not at all prejudiced against her on *that* account.

MRS MALAPROP

You are very good, and very considerate, Captain. I am   30
sure I have done everything in my power since I exploded the affair! Long ago I laid my positive conjunctions on her never to think on the fellow again. I have since laid Sir Anthony's preposition before her, but I'm sorry to say she

---

13 *ineffectual* for, intellectual
15 *flower of beauty* 76 (flower, beauty, 75)
19 *fruit* 76 (fruits 75)
20 *specious* deceptively attractive
23 *pineapple* for, pinnacle
25–6 *beggarly, strolling, eavesdropping* poor, wandering, fortune-hunter ('eavesdropping' because he listens out to hear of someone wealthy to marry)
28 *silly* insignificant
31 *exploded* for, exposed
32 *conjunctions* 76 (conjunction 75), for, injunctions
34 *preposition* for, proposition

seems resolved to decline every particle that I enjoin her.   35

ABSOLUTE

It must be very distressing indeed, ma'am.

MRS MALAPROP

O, it gives me the hydrostatics to such a degree! I thought
she had persisted from corresponding with him; but,
behold, this very day, I have interceded another letter from
the fellow! I believe I have it in my pocket.   40

ABSOLUTE

(*Aside*) O the devil! My last note.

MRS MALAPROP

Ay, here it is.

ABSOLUTE

(*Aside*) Ay, my note indeed! O the little traitress Lucy.

MRS MALAPROP

There, perhaps you may know the writing. (*Gives him the
letter*)

ABSOLUTE

I think I have seen the hand before. Yes, I *certainly must*   45
have seen this hand before.

MRS MALAPROP

Nay, but read it, Captain.

ABSOLUTE

(*Reads*) 'My soul's idol, my adored Lydia!' Very tender
indeed!

MRS MALAPROP

Tender! Ay, and prophane too, o' my conscience!   50

ABSOLUTE

'I am excessively alarmed at the intelligence you send me,
the more so, as my new rival –'

MRS MALAPROP

That's *you*, sir.

---

35   *decline* refuse
     particle for, article (all the preceding malapropisms – 'conjunctions', 'preposition', 'decline'
     and 'particle' – have been grammatical terms)
     enjoin command
37   *O* 76 (om. 75)
     hydrostatics the science of weighing fluids; for, hysterics
38   *persisted* for, desisted
39   *interceded* for, intercepted

ABSOLUTE

'– has universally the character of being an accomplished
gentleman and a man of honour.' Well, that's handsome   55
enough.

MRS MALAPROP

O, the fellow has some design in writing so.

ABSOLUTE

That he had, I'll answer for him, ma'am.

MRS MALAPROP

But go on, sir; you'll see presently.

ABSOLUTE

'As for the old weather-beaten she-dragon who guards   60
you –' Who can he mean by that?

MRS MALAPROP

Me, sir, *me*; he means *me* there – what do you think now?
But go on a little further.

ABSOLUTE

Impudent scoundrel! '– it shall go hard but I will elude
her vigilance, as I am told that the same ridiculous   65
vanity, which makes her dress up her coarse features
and deck her dull chat with hard words which she don't
understand –'

MRS MALAPROP

There, sir! An attack upon my language! What do you
think of that? An aspersion upon my parts of speech! Was   70
ever such a brute! Sure if I reprehend anything in this
world, it is the use of my oracular tongue, and a nice
derangement of epitaphs!

ABSOLUTE

He deserves to be hanged and quartered! Let me see '–
same ridiculous vanity –'   75

MRS MALAPROP

You need not read it again, sir.

ABSOLUTE

I beg pardon, ma'am, '– does also lay her open to the

57   *has* 76 (had 75)
64–5   *elude her vigilance* escape her watchfulness
71   *reprehend* for, apprehend
72   *oracular* speaking ambiguously like an oracle; for, vernacular
73   *derangement of epitaphs* for, arrangement of epithets

grossest deceptions from flattery and pretended admiration –'
an impudent coxcomb! '– so that I have a scheme to
see you shortly with the old harridan's consent, and   80
even to make her a go-between in our interviews.' Was ever
such assurance!

MRS MALAPROP

Did you ever hear anything like it? He'll elude my
vigilance, will he? Yes, yes! Ha, ha! He's very likely to
enter these doors! We'll try who can plot best!   85

ABSOLUTE

So we will, ma'am; so we will. Ha, ha, ha! A conceited
puppy. Ha, ha, ha! Well, but, Mrs Malaprop, as the girl
seems so infatuated by this fellow, suppose you were to
wink at her corresponding with him for a little time? Let
her even plot an elopement with him. Then do you   90
connive at her escape, while I, just in the nick, will have
the fellow laid by the heels, and fairly contrive to carry her
off in his stead.

MRS MALAPROP

I am delighted with the scheme – never was anything better
perpetrated!   95

ABSOLUTE

But, pray, could not I see the lady for a few minutes now?
I should like to try her temper a little.

MRS MALAPROP

Why, I don't know: I doubt she is not prepared for a visit
of this kind. There is a decorum in these matters.

ABSOLUTE

O Lord! she won't mind *me*. Only tell her Beverley –   100

MRS MALAPROP

Sir!

ABSOLUTE

(*Aside*) Gently, good tongue.

MRS MALAPROP

What did you say of Beverley?

82 *assurance* presumption
86 *So we will, ma'am; so we will.* 76 (om. 75)
91 *in the nick* in the nick of time, just in time
92 *laid by the heels* captured, thwarted
97 *try her temper* test her mood
98 *a visit* 76 (a first visit 75)

ABSOLUTE

O, I was going to propose that you should tell her, by way
of jest, that it was Beverley who was below. She'd come   105
down fast enough then. Ha, ha, ha!

MRS MALAPROP

'Twould be a trick she well deserves. Besides, you know,
the fellow tells her he'll get my consent to see her. Ha,
ha! Let him, if he can, I say again. (*Calling*) Lydia,
come down here! [*To* ABSOLUTE] He'll make me a   110
'go-between in their interviews'! Ha, ha, ha! [*Calling*]
Come down, I say, Lydia! [*To* ABSOLUTE] I don't
wonder at your laughing. Ha, ha, ha! His impudence is truly
ridiculous.

ABSOLUTE

'Tis very ridiculous, upon my soul, ma'am. Ha, ha, ha!   115

MRS MALAPROP

The little hussy won't hear. Well, I'll go and tell her at
once who it is. She shall know that Captain Absolute is
come to wait on her. And I'll make her behave as becomes
a young woman.

ABSOLUTE

As you please, ma'am.   120

MRS MALAPROP

For the present, Captain, your servant. Ah, you've not done
laughing yet, I see. 'Elude my vigilance'! Yes, yes.
Ha, ha, ha!   *Exit*

ABSOLUTE

Ha, ha, ha! One would think now that I might throw off all
disguise at once, and seize my prize with security – but   125
such is Lydia's caprice, that to undeceive were probably to
lose her. I'll see whether she knows me.

(*Walks aside, and seems engaged in looking at the pictures*)

Enter LYDIA [LANGUISH]

LYDIA

[*Aside*] What a scene am I now to go through! Surely
nothing can be more dreadful than to be obliged to listen
to the loathsome addresses of a stranger to one's heart. I   130
have heard of girls persecuted as I am, who have appealed
in behalf of their favoured lover to the generosity of his

rival. Suppose I were to try it? There stands the hated
rival – an officer too! But, O, how unlike my Beverley! I
wonder he don't begin – truly he seems a very negligent   135
wooer! Quite at his ease, upon my word! I'll speak first.
[*Calls*] Mr Absolute!

ABSOLUTE

Madam.   (*Turns round*)

LYDIA

O Heavens! Beverley!

ABSOLUTE

Hush! Hush, my life! Softly! Be not surprised!   140

LYDIA

I am so astonished! And so terrified! And so overjoyed!
For heaven's sake, how came you here?

ABSOLUTE

Briefly: I have deceived your aunt. I was informed that
my new rival was to visit here this evening, and,
contriving to have him kept away, have passed myself on   145
her for Captain Absolute.

LYDIA

O, charming! And she really takes you for young Absolute?

ABSOLUTE

O, she's convinced of it.

LYDIA

Ha, ha, ha! I can't forbear laughing to think how her
sagacity is overreached!   150

ABSOLUTE

But we trifle with our precious moments. Such another
opportunity may not occur. Then let me now conjure my
kind, my condescending angel, to fix the time when I
may rescue her from undeserved persecution, and, with a
licensed warmth, plead for my reward.   155

LYDIA

Will you then, Beverley, consent to forfeit that portion of

---

143 *Briefly* In brief
153 *condescending* accommodating
155 *licensed* permitted (because they will be married)
156 *portion* share

my paltry wealth? That burden on the wings of love?

ABSOLUTE

O come to me, rich only thus – in loveliness. Bring no
portion to me but thy love; 'twill be generous in you,
Lydia, for well you know, it is the only dower your poor   160
Beverley can repay.

LYDIA

[*Aside*] How persuasive are his words! How charming
will poverty be with him!

ABSOLUTE

Ah, my soul, what a life will we then live? Love shall be
our idol and support! We will worship him with a monastic   165
strictness, abjuring all worldly toys to centre every
thought and action there. Proud of calamity, we will enjoy
the wreck of wealth, while the surrounding gloom of
adversity shall make the flame of our pure love show
doubly bright. By heavens! I would fling all goods of   170
fortune from me with a prodigal hand to enjoy the scene
where I might clasp my Lydia to my bosom, and say,
(*Embrac*[*ing*] *her*) 'The world affords no smile to me but
here'. (*Aside*) If she holds out now the devil is in it!

LYDIA

Now could I fly with him to the Antipodes! But my   175
persecution is not yet come to a crisis.

Enter MRS MALAPROP, *listening*

MRS MALAPROP

(*Aside*) I'm impatient to know how the little hussy
deports herself.

ABSOLUTE

So pensive, Lydia! Is then your warmth abated?

MRS MALAPROP

[*Aside*] 'Warmth abated'! So! She has been in a passion, I   180
suppose.

---

157 *burden* 76 (burthen 75)
     That burden on the wings of love Lydia, and later Absolute, take on the language of the
     sentimental novels Lydia reads
160 *dower* dowry, marriage portion
166 *toys* trifles
173 s.d *Embraces* ed. (*embracing* 75, 76)
175 *Antipodes* opposite side of the earth

LYDIA

No, nor ever can while I have life.

MRS MALAPROP

[*Aside*] An ill-tempered little devil! She'll be in a passion 'all her life' will she?

LYDIA

Think not the idle threats of my ridiculous aunt can ever   185
have any weight with me.

MRS MALAPROP

[*Aside*] Very dutiful, upon my word!

LYDIA

Let her choice be Captain Absolute, but Beverley is mine.

MRS MALAPROP

[*Aside*] I am astonished at her assurance! *To his face* – this is to his
face!   190

ABSOLUTE

Thus, then, (*Kneeling*) let me enforce my suit.

MRS MALAPROP

[*Aside*] Ay, poor young man! Down on his knees entreating
for pity! I can contain no longer. [*To* LYDIA] Why, thou
vixen! I have overheard you.

ABSOLUTE

(*Aside*) O confound her vigilance! [*Rises*]   195

MRS MALAPROP

Captain Absolute, I know not how to apologize for her
shocking rudeness.

ABSOLUTE

(*Aside*) So all's safe, I find. [*To* MRS MALAPROP] I have
hopes, madam, that time will bring the young lady –

MRS MALAPROP

O, there's nothing to be hoped for from her! She's as   200
headstrong as an allegory on the banks of Nile.

LYDIA

Nay, madam, what do you charge me with now?

MRS MALAPROP

Why, thou   unblushing   rebel,   didn't   you   tell   this

---

189   *this is to* 76 (this to 75)
193–4   *thou vixen* 76 (hussy, hussy 75)
201   *allegory* for, alligator

gentleman to his face that you loved another better? Didn't
you say you never would be his?　　　205

LYDIA

No, madam, I did not.

MRS MALAPROP

Good heavens! What assurance! Lydia, Lydia, you ought
to know that lying don't become a young woman! Didn't
you boast that Beverley – that stroller, Beverley –
possessed your heart? Tell me that, I say.　　　210

LYDIA

'Tis true, ma'am, and none but Beverley –

MRS MALAPROP

Hold; hold, assurance! You shall not be so rude.

ABSOLUTE

Nay, pray, Mrs Malaprop, don't stop the young lady's
speech. She's very welcome to talk thus – it does not hurt
me in the least, I assure you.　　　215

MRS MALAPROP

You are *too* good, Captain, *too* amiably patient. But come
with me, miss. Let us see you again soon, Captain.
Remember what we have fixed.

ABSOLUTE

I shall, ma'am.

MRS MALAPROP

Come, take a graceful leave of the gentleman.　　　220

LYDIA

May every blessing wait on my Beverley, my loved Bev –

MRS MALAPROP

Hussy! I'll choke the word in your throat! Come along,
come along.

> *Exeunt severally,* [ABSOLUTE] *kissing his hand to*
> LYDIA, MRS MALAPROP *stopping her from speaking*

[Act III,] Scene iv

[BOB] ACRES's *lodgings*

[BOB] ACRES *as just dressed and* DAVID

ACRES

Indeed, David, do you think I become it so?

DAVID

You are quite another creature, believe me, master, by the mass! An we've any luck, we shall see the Devon monkeyrony in all the print-shops in Bath!

ACRES

Dress *does* make a difference, David.   5

DAVID

'Tis all in all, I think. Difference! Why, an you were to go now to Clod Hall, I am certain the old lady wouldn't know you. Master Butler wouldn't believe his own eyes, and Mrs Pickle would cry 'Lard preserve me!' Our dairymaid would come giggling to the door, and I   10 warrant Dolly Tester, your honour's favourite, would blush like my waistcoat. Oons! I'll hold a gallon there a'n't a dog in the house but would bark, and I question whether *Phyllis* would wag a hair of her tail!

---

0   s.d. 2 ed. ('*Acres and David*'; '*Acres as just dress'd*' 75, 76)

1   *become it so* look so good in it

3   *An* If

4   *monkeyrony* David's corruption of 'macaroni', a fashionable man or fop
    print-shops shops which sold prints and engravings including pictures of contemporary famous people

7   *Clod Hall* the name of Acres' Devonshire house – from 'clod', a lump of earth (Bob is out of place in sophisticated Bath society)
    old lady Bob's mother

9   *Mrs Pickle* the cook

11   *Dolly Tester* A tester-bed had a canopy – so Dolly is probably a chambermaid. Alternatively, a tester was sixpence – perhaps this was what the 'favourite' charged for bedroom services.

12   *Oons!* An oath, from 'God's wounds'

12–13   *hold a gallon . . . bark* bet a gallon (of ale) there isn't a dog there that would bark (i.e. recognise you)

14   *Phyllis* Bob's favourite hunting-dog (see IV.i.67)

ACRES

Ay, David, there's nothing like *polishing*.　　15

DAVID

So I says of your honour's boots, but the boy never heeds me!

ACRES

But, David, has Mr De la Grace been here? I must rub up my balancing, and chasing, and boring.

DAVID

I'll call again, sir.　　20

ACRES

Do, and see if there are any letters for me at the post-office.

DAVID

I will. By the mass, I can't help looking at your head! If I hadn't been by at the cooking, I wish I may die if I should have known the dish again myself!　　*Exit*

ACRES

(*Com[ing] forward, practising a dancing step*)　　25 Sink, slide, coupee. Confound the first inventors of cotillions, say I! They are as bad as algebra to us country gentlemen. I can walk a minuet easy enough when I'm forced! And I have been accounted a good stick in a country-dance. Od's jigs and tabors, I never valued your　　30 cross-over to couple, figure in, right and left; and I'd foot it with e'er a captain in the county! But these outlandish heathen allemandes and cotillions are quite beyond me!

---

18 *De la Grace* The name means 'of social poise' (French). De la Grace is the dancing master.

19 *balancing, and chasing, and boring* dancing-terms from the French: 'balancer', to sway from one foot to the other; 'chassé', gliding; 'bourrée', a lively dance in three-quarter time

26 *Sink, slide, coupee* more dancing terms; bending the knees, stepping smoothly to one side, and resting on one foot, pass the other forward or backward and bow to your partner

29 *good stick* (here) good dancer

30 *valued* appreciated
   tabors small drums

31 *cross-over . . . left* movements in country-dancing
   to 76 (two 75)
   foot dance

32 *e'er a* any

33 *allemandes* lively German dances

I shall never prosper at 'em, that's sure. Mine are true-born
English legs; they don't understand their cursed French   35
lingo! Their *pas* this, and *pas* that, and *pas* t'other! Damn
me, my feet don't like to be called paws! No, 'tis certain I
have most antigallican toes!

Enter SERVANT

SERVANT
Here is Sir Lucius O'Trigger to wait on you, sir.
ACRES
Show him in.   40

[*Exit* SERVANT]

Enter SIR LUCIUS [O'TRIGGER]

SIR LUCIUS
Mr Acres, I am delighted to embrace you.
ACRES
My dear Sir Lucius, I kiss your hands.
SIR LUCIUS
Pray, my friend, what has brought you so suddenly to
Bath?
ACRES
Faith, I have followed Cupid's jack-o'-lantern, and find   45
myself in a quagmire at last. In short, I have been very
ill-used, Sir Lucius. I don't choose to mention names, but
look on me as a very ill-used gentleman.
SIR LUCIUS
Pray, what is the case? I ask no names.
ACRES
Mark me, Sir Lucius. I fall as deep as need be in love   50
with a young lady. Her friends take my part; I follow her to
Bath, send word of my arrival, and receive answer that
the lady is to be otherwise disposed of. This, Sir Lucius,
I call being ill-used.

36 *lingo* language (slang)
    pas pronounced 'paws' by Acres; French either for 'step' or 'no'
38 *antigallican* anti-French
45–6 *Cupid's jack-o'-lantern . . . quagmire* Cupid was the god of love in classical mythology;
    the jack-o'-lantern was otherwise known as the 'ignis fatuus' or 'will-o'-the-wisp', a flame
    produced by marsh gas which misleads travellers in the night.
50 *fall* 76 (falls 75)

SIR LUCIUS

Very ill, upon my conscience. Pray, can you divine the   55
cause of it?

ACRES

Why, there's the matter. She has another lover, *one*
Beverley, who, I am told, is now in Bath. Od's slanders
and lies, he must be at the bottom of it.

SIR LUCIUS

A rival in the case, is there? And you think he has   60
supplanted you unfairly.

ACRES

Unfairly! To be sure he has. He never could have done it
fairly.

SIR LUCIUS

Then, sure, you know what is to be done!

ACRES

Not I, upon my soul!   65

SIR LUCIUS

We wear no swords here, but you understand me.

ACRES

What! Fight him!

SIR LUCIUS

Ay, to be sure. What can I mean else?

ACRES

But he has given me no provocation.

SIR LUCIUS

Now, I think he has given you the greatest provocation in   70
the world. Can a man commit a more heinous offence
against another than to fall in love with the same woman?
O, by my soul, it is the most unpardonable breach of
friendship!

ACRES

Breach of *friendship*, ay, ay; but I have no acquaintance   75
with this man. I never saw him in my life.

SIR LUCIUS

That's no argument at all. He has the less right then to take
such a liberty.

66 *wear no swords here* Wearing swords, and the duelling that that might give rise to, was
    forbidden at Bath by rules set down by Beau Nash.
71 *heinous* atrocious

ACRES

 Gad, that's true. I grow full of anger, Sir Lucius! I fire
apace! Od's hilts and blades, I find a man may have a   80
deal of valour in him, and not know it! But couldn't I
contrive to have a little right of my side?

SIR LUCIUS

 What the devil signifies *right*, when your *honour* is
concerned? Do you think *Achilles*, or my little *Alexander
the Great* ever inquired where the right lay? No, by my   85
soul, they drew their broadswords, and left the lazy sons
of peace to settle the justice of it.

ACRES

 Your words are a grenadier's march to my heart! I believe
courage must be catching! I certainly do feel a kind of
valour rising as it were – a kind of courage, as I may say.   90
Od's flints, pans, and triggers! I'll challenge him directly.

SIR LUCIUS

 Ah, my little friend! If we had Blunderbuss Hall here, I
could show you a range of ancestry, in the O'Trigger line,
that would furnish the New Room, every one of whom had
killed his man! For though the mansion-house and dirty   95
acres have slipped through my fingers, I thank heaven our
honour, and the family-pictures, are as fresh as ever.

<hr/>

 79 *Gad* 'God'
79–80 *fire apace* grow angry quickly
 82 *of my side* on my side
 84 *Achilles* the champion of the Greeks in the Trojan War
84–5 *little Alexander the Great* 'little' is an affectionate joke at the expense of the actor who
   originally played Acres, John Quick, who was notoriously short; Alexander the Great was
   a famous warrior king of Macedonia (356–323 BC).
 86 *broadswords* wide-bladed swords, used for slashing rather than thrusting
 88 *a grenadier's march* Sir Lucius' references to Alexander may have brought Acres in mind
   of the song 'The British Grenadiers': 'Some talk of Alexander and some of Hercules . . .'
 91 *pans* the part of a firearm that held the gunpowder
 92 *Blunderbuss Hall* the name of Sir Lucius O'Trigger's family home in Ireland. A blunderbuss is a short gun with a large bore that can fire many balls at once, also – for obvious
   reasons – a noisy blusterer.
 94 *New Room* the Upper Assembly Rooms in Bath, situated east of the Circus, and built by
   John Wood. They were opened in 1771, and Sheridan wrote humorous verses to celebrate
   the occasion, published in *The Bath Chronicle*, Oct. 1771.
95–6 *dirty acres* given the name of Sir Lucius' interlocutor, the choice of words is (perhaps
   deliberately) unfortunate
 96 *heaven* 76 (God 75)

ACRES

O, Sir Lucius, I have had ancestors too! Every man of 'em
Colonel or Captain in the militia! Od's balls and barrels,
say no more! I'm braced for it. The thunder of your words　　100
has soured the milk of human kindness in my breast!
Zounds, as the man in the play says, 'I could do such
deeds!'

SIR LUCIUS

Come, come, there must be no passion at all in the case.
These things should always be done civilly.　　105

ACRES

I must be in a passion, Sir Lucius, I must be in a rage. Dear
Sir Lucius, let me be in a rage, if you love me. Come, here's
pen and paper. (*Sits down to write*) I would the ink were red!
Indite, I say, indite! How shall I begin? Od's bullets and
blades! I'll write a good bold hand, however.　　110

SIR LUCIUS

Pray compose yourself.

ACRES

Come. Now shall I begin with an oath? Do, Sir Lucius, let me
begin with a damme.

SIR LUCIUS

Foh, foh! Do the thing *decently* and like a Christian.
Begin now. 'Sir –'　　115

ACRES

That's too civil by half.

SIR LUCIUS

'– To prevent the confusion that might arise –'

ACRES

Well.

SIR LUCIUS

'– from our both addressing the same lady –'

99　*balls and barrels* bullets and gun-barrels
100　*for it* 76 (75 continues: my nerves are become catgut! My sinews, wire! And my heart, pinchbeck!)
101　*the milk of human kindness* cf. Lady Macbeth in Shakespeare's *Macbeth* who fears her husband's nature is 'too full o'th'milk of human kindness / To catch the nearest way' (I.iv.16–17)
102–3　*the man . . . deeds* It is Shakespeare's King Lear himself who says 'I will do such things –', he goes on, 'what they are yet, I know not' (*Lear*, II.ii.464–6)
109　*Indite* Write down
113　*damme* for 'damn me' (cf. II.i.313–4)

ACRES

Ay, there's the reason: 'same lady'. Well?   120

SIR LUCIUS

'– I shall expect the honour of your company –'

ACRES

Zounds, I'm not asking him to dinner.

SIR LUCIUS

Pray be easy.

ACRES

Well then, '– honour of your company –'

SIR LUCIUS

'– to settle our pretensions –'   125

ACRES

Well.

SIR LUCIUS

Let me see. Ay, Kingsmead Fields will do. '– in
Kingsmead Fields.'

ACRES

So that's done. Well, I'll fold it up presently; my own
crest – a hand and dagger – shall be the seal.   130

SIR LUCIUS

You see now: this little explanation will put a stop at once
to all confusion or misunderstanding that might arise
between you.

ACRES

Ay, we fight to prevent any misunderstanding.

SIR LUCIUS

Now, I'll leave you to fix your own time. Take my   135
advice, and you'll decide it this evening if you can; then,
let the worst come of it, 'twill be off your mind tomorrow.

ACRES

Very true.

SIR LUCIUS

So I shall see nothing more of you, unless it be by letter,
till the evening. I would do myself the honour to carry   140

123   *be easy* stage Irish meaning 'don't be so eager'
125   *pretensions* (competing) claims
127   *Kingsmead Fields* open country to the west of Bath, by Kingsmead Street where Sheri-
        dan lodged
130   *crest . . . seal* family coat of arms (on a ring) shall be pressed into the wax that secures
        the letter

your message; but, to tell you a secret, I believe I shall
have just such another affair on my own hands. There is
a gay Captain here, who put a jest on me lately, at the
expense of my country, and I only want to fall in with the
gentleman, to call him out.   145

ACRES

By my valour, I should like to see you fight first! Od's
life, I should like to see you kill him, if it was only to
get a little lesson.

SIR LUCIUS

I shall be very proud of instructing you. Well, for the
present. But remember now, when you meet your   150
antagonist, do everything in a mild and agreeable
manner. Let your courage be as keen, but at the same
time as polished, as your sword.

Exeunt severally

Act IV, Scene i

[BOB] ACRES's *Lodgings*

[BOB] ACRES *and* DAVID

DAVID

Then, by the mass, sir, I would do no such thing. Ne'er a
Sir Lucius O'Trigger in the kingdom should make me
fight, when I wa'n't so minded. Oons, what will the old
lady say, when she hears o't?

ACRES

Ah, David, if you had heard Sir Lucius! Od's sparks and   5
flames, he would have roused your valour.

DAVID

Not he, indeed. I hates such bloodthirsty cormorants.
Look'ee, Master, if you'd wanted a bout at boxing,

143–4 *at the expense of my country* to the detriment of Ireland
144 *fall in with* meet

7 *cormorants* seabirds thought to be insatiable; here a metaphor for people whose appetite
for fighting is as voracious as the birds' for food

quarterstaff, or short-staff, I should never be the man
to bid you cry off. But for your cursed sharps and snaps,   10
I never knew any good come of 'em.

ACRES

But my *honour*, David, my *honour*! I must be very careful
of my honour.

DAVID

Ay, by the mass! And I would be very careful of it, and I
think in return my *honour* couldn't do less than to be very   15
careful of *me*.

ACRES

Od's blades, David, no gentleman will ever risk the loss
of his honour!

DAVID

I say then, it would be but civil in *honour* never to risk the
loss of a *gentleman*. Look'ee, Master, this *honour* seems   20
to me to be a marvellous false friend; ay, truly, a very
courtier-like servant. Put the case I was a gentleman,
which, thank God, no one can say of me. Well, my honour
makes me quarrel with another gentleman of my
acquaintance. So we fight. Pleasant enough, that. Boh!   25
I kill him, the more's my luck. Now, pray, who gets the
profit of it? Why, my *honour*. But put the case that he
kills me! By the mass! I go to the worms, and my honour
whips over to my enemy!

ACRES

No, David; in that case, od's crowns and laurels, your   30
honour follows you to the grave.

DAVID

Now, that's just the place where I could make a shift to do
without it.

9 *quarterstaff, or short-staff* heavy pole tipped with iron or a similar but smaller weapon
    (both peasants' arms)
10 *sharps and snaps* duelling swords and pistols (for the snapping sound made when fired)
20 *a gentleman* 76 (the gentleman 75)
22 *courtier-like* Attendants at court were proverbially unreliable.
23–33 These exchanges about honour recall Falstaff's soliloquy (*I Henry IV*, V.i.127–40): 'Can hon-
    our set to a leg? No. Or an arm? No . . . What is honour? A word . . . Who hath it? He that
    died o'Wednesday. Doth he feel it? No . . . I'll none of it. Honour is a mere scutcheon . . .'
25 *Boh!* an exclamation intended to startle
28–9 *I go to the worms . . . over to* I die and am buried and my honour transfers to
32 *make a shift* manage

ACRES

Zounds, David, you're a coward! It doesn't become my
valour to listen to you. What, shall I disgrace my   35
ancestors? Think of that, David, think what it would be
to disgrace my ancestors!

DAVID

Under favour, the surest way of not disgracing them is to
keep as long as you can out of their company. Look'ee
now, master, to go to them in such haste, with an ounce   40
of lead in your brains, I should think might as well be let
alone. Our ancestors are very good kind of folks; but they
are the last people I should choose to have a visiting
acquaintance with.

ACRES

But, David, now, you don't think there is such very,   45
very, *very* great danger, hey? Od's life, people often
fight without any mischief done!

DAVID

By the mass, I think 'tis ten to one against you! Oons, here
to meet some lion-headed fellow, I warrant, with his
damned double-barrelled swords, and cut-and-thrust   50
pistols! Lord bless us, it makes me tremble to think o't!
Those be such desperate bloody-minded weapons! Well,
I never could abide 'em! From a child I never could fancy
'em! I suppose there a'n't so merciless a beast in the world
as your loaded pistol!   55

ACRES

Zounds! I *won't* be afraid. Od's fire and fury! You shan't
make me afraid. Here is the challenge, and I have sent for
my dear friend Jack Absolute to carry it for me.

DAVID

Ay, i'the name of mischief, let *him* be the messenger. For
my part, I wouldn't lend a hand to it for the best horse in   60

---

38 *Under favour* With your permission
40–41 *an ounce of lead* i.e. a bullet
50–1 *double-barrelled swords, and cut-and-thrust pistols* David puts the adjectives with the
wrong nouns.

your stable. By the mass, it don't look like another letter!
It is, as I may say, a designing and malicious-looking
letter, and, I warrant, smells of gunpowder like a soldier's
pouch! Oons! I wouldn't swear it mayn't go off!

ACRES

Out, you poltroon! You ha'n't the valour of a grasshopper.   65

DAVID

Well, I say no more. 'Twill be sad news, to be sure, at
Clod Hall! But I ha' done. How Phyllis will howl when
she hears of it! Ay, poor bitch, she little thinks what
shooting her master's going after! (*Whimpering*) And I
warrant old Crop, who has carried your honour, field and   70
road, these ten years, will curse the hour he was born.

ACRES

It won't do, David, I am determined to fight – so get along,
you coward, while I'm in the mind.

Enter SERVANT

SERVANT

Captain Absolute, sir.

ACRES

O, show him up.   75

Exit SERVANT

DAVID

Well, heaven send we be all alive this time tomorrow.

ACRES

What's that! Don't provoke me, David!

DAVID

(*Whimpering*) Goodbye, master.

ACRES

Get along, you cowardly, dastardly, croaking raven.

Exit DAVID

63–4 *soldier's pouch* bag in which a soldier carried gunpowder
  65 *poltroon* coward
  70 *old Crop* Acres' horse
  79 *croaking raven* ravens were proverbially symbols of bad fortune; the 'croaking raven'
       recalls Lady Macbeth's 'The raven ... / That croaks the fatal entrance of Duncan / Under
       my battlements '(*Macbeth*, I.v.36–9).

Enter [JACK] ABSOLUTE

ABSOLUTE

What's the matter, Bob?   80

ACRES

A vile, sheep-hearted blockhead! If I hadn't the valour of
St George and the dragon to boot –

ABSOLUTE

But what did you want with me, Bob?

ACRES

O! There.   (*Gives him the challenge*)

ABSOLUTE

'To Ensign Beverley.' (*Aside*) So, what's going on now!   85
[*To* ACRES] Well, what's this?

ACRES

A challenge!

ABSOLUTE

Indeed! Why, you won't fight him, will you, Bob?

ACRES

Egad, but I will, Jack. Sir Lucius has wrought me to it. He
has left me full of rage, and I'll fight this evening, that so   90
much good passion mayn't be wasted.

ABSOLUTE

But what have I to do with this?

ACRES

Why, as I think you know something of this fellow, I
want you to find him out for me, and give him this
mortal *defiance*.   95

ABSOLUTE

Well, give it to me, and trust me he gets it.

ACRES

Thank you, my dear friend, my dear Jack; but it is giving
you a great deal of trouble.

ABSOLUTE

Not in the least: I beg you won't mention it. No trouble in
the world, I assure you.   100

82 *St George and the dragon* legendary (military) patron saint of England who bravely killed
    a dragon
    to boot in addition
89 *wrought me to it* worked me up to it
95 *mortal defiance* challenge to the death

ACRES

You are very kind. What it is to have a friend! You couldn't be my second could you, Jack?

ABSOLUTE

Why, no, Bob, not in *this* affair: it would not be quite so proper.

ACRES

Well, then, I must get my friend Sir Lucius. I shall have   105
your good wishes, however, Jack.

ABSOLUTE

Whenever he meets you, believe me.

Enter SERVANT

SERVANT

Sir Anthony Absolute is below inquiring for the Captain.

ABSOLUTE

I'll come instantly. Well, my little hero, success attend
you.   *Going*   110

ACRES

Stay, stay, Jack. If Beverly should ask you what kind of a
man your friend Acres is, do tell him I am a devil of a
fellow, will you, Jack?

ABSOLUTE

To be sure I shall. I'll say you are a determined dog, hey,
Bob!   115

ACRES

Ay, do, do. And if that frightens him, egad, perhaps he
mayn't come. So tell him I generally kill a man a week,
will you, Jack!

ABSOLUTE

I will, I will; I'll say you are called in the country
'Fighting Bob!'   120

ACRES

Right, right. 'Tis all to prevent mischief; for I don't want
to take his life if I clear my honour.

ABSOLUTE

No! That's very kind of you.

102   *second* friend and supporter in a duel who saw to it that there was fair play
103–4   *not be quite so proper* (1) because Beverley is supposed to be his friend; (2) because he
          would be acting against a fellow officer; (3) because he would be acting against himself
105   *get* 76 (fix on 75)

[124]

ACRES

Why, you don't wish me to kill him, do you, Jack?

ABSOLUTE

No, upon my soul, I do not. But a devil of a fellow, hey?   125

Going

ACRES

True, true. But stay, stay, Jack: you may add that you never saw me in such a rage before – a most devouring rage!

ABSOLUTE

I will, I will.

ACRES

Remember, Jack – a determined dog!

ABSOLUTE

Ay, ay, 'Fighting Bob'!   130

Exeunt severally

[Act IV,] Scene ii

MRS MALAPROP'*s lodgings*

MRS MALAPROP *and* LYDIA [LANGUISH]

MRS MALAPROP

Why, thou perverse one! Tell me what you can object to him? Isn't he a handsome man? Tell me that. A genteel man? A pretty figure of a man?

LYDIA

(*Aside*) She little thinks whom she is praising! [*To* MRS MALAPROP] So is Beverley, ma'am.   5

MRS MALAPROP

No caparisons, miss, if you please! Caparisons don't become a young woman. No! Captain Absolute is indeed a fine gentleman!

LYDIA

(*Aside*) Ay, the Captain Absolute *you* have seen.

6 *caparisons* ornamental saddle-cloths for horses; for, comparisons

MRS MALAPROP

Then he's *so* well bred, *so* full of alacrity, and adulation!   10
And has *so much* to say for himself – in such good language
too! His physiognomy so grammatical! Then his presence
is so noble! I protest, when I saw him, I thought of what
Hamlet says in the play: 'Hesperian curls! The front of *Job*
himself! An eye, like *March*, to threaten at command! A   15
station, like Harry Mercury, new –' Something about
kissing on a hill. However, the similitude struck me directly.

LYDIA

(*Aside*) How enraged she'll be presently when she discovers
her mistake!

Enter SERVANT

SERVANT

Sir Anthony and Captain Absolute are below, ma'am.   20

MRS MALAPROP

Show them up here.

Exit SERVANT

Now, Lydia, I insist on you behaving as becomes a young
woman. Show your good breeding at least, though you
have forgot your duty.

LYDIA

Madam, I have told you my resolution: I shall not only give   25
him no encouragement, but I won't even speak to, or look
at him.   (*Flings herself into a chair, with her face from the door*)

10 *adulation* for, admiration
12 *physiognomy* the face as an indication of character; for, phraseology
14–17 Hamlet's actual speech, a description of his dead father, reads: 'See what a grace was
      seated on this brow – / Hyperion's curls, the front of Jove himself, / An eye like Mars, to
      threaten or command, / A station like the herald Mercury / New lighted on a heaven-
      kissing hill; / A combination and a form indeed / Where every god did seem to set his
      seal / To give the world assurance of a man' (III.iv.54–61).
14 *Hesperian* a poetic adjective meaning 'western'; for, Hyperion (see above) who, in clas-
      sical mythology, was the father of the sun and moon
      Job an Old Testament figure put by God through many trials in the Bible; for, Jove (see
      above) the king of the gods
15 *March* for, Mars (the god of war)
16 *station* posture
      Harry Mercury a name; for, herald Mercury (see above), in classical mythology the winged
      messenger ('herald') of the gods
17 *similitude* for, similarity or simile

Enter SIR ANTHONY [ABSOLUTE] *and*
[JACK] ABSOLUTE

SIR ANTHONY

Here we are, Mrs Malaprop, come to mitigate the frowns
of unrelenting beauty; and difficulty enough I had to bring
this fellow. I don't know what's the matter, but if I hadn't   30
held him by force, he'd have given me the slip.

MRS MALAPROP

You have infinite trouble, Sir Anthony, in the affair. I am
ashamed for the cause! (*Aside to* LYDIA) Lydia, Lydia,
rise I beseech you! Pay your respects!

SIR ANTHONY

I hope, madam, that Miss Languish has reflected on the   35
worth of this gentleman, and the regard due to her aunt's
choice, and *my* alliance. (*Aside to* ABSOLUTE) Now,
Jack, speak to her!

ABSOLUTE

(*Aside*) What the devil shall I do? [*To* SIR ANTONY]
You see, sir, she won't even look at me whilst you are   40
here. I knew she wouldn't! I told you so. Let me entreat
you, sir, to leave us together!

Seems to expostulate with [SIR ANTONY]

LYDIA

(*Aside*) I wonder I ha'n't heard my aunt exclaim yet! Sure
she can't have looked at him! Perhaps their regimentals
are alike – and she is something blind.   45

SIR ANTHONY

I say, sir, I won't stir a foot yet.

MRS MALAPROP

I am sorry to say, Sir Anthony, that my affluence over my
niece is very small. (*Aside to* [LYDIA]) Turn round, Lydia.
I blush for you!

---

37 *my alliance* joining with my family (by marriage)
42 s.d. ed. (*Absolute seems to expostulate with his Father* 75, 76)
44 *regimentals* military uniforms
45 *something* somewhat
47 *affluence* for, influence
48, 55, 70 s.d. ed. (*Aside to her* 75, 76)

SIR ANTHONY

May I not flatter myself that Miss Languish will assign   50
what cause of dislike she can have to my son! (*Aside to*
[ABSOLUTE]) Why don't you begin, Jack? Speak, you
puppy, speak!

MRS MALAPROP

It is impossible, Sir Anthony, she can have any. She will
not *say* she has. (*Aside to* [LYDIA]) Answer, hussy! Why   55
don't you answer?

SIR ANTHONY

Then, madam, I trust that a childish and hasty predilection
will be no bar to Jack's happiness. (*Aside to* [ABSOLUTE])
Zounds, sirrah! Why don't you speak?

LYDIA

(*Aside*) I think my lover seems as little inclined to   60
conversation as myself. How strangely blind my aunt
must be!

ABSOLUTE

Hem, hem! Madam – hem! (*Attempts to speak, then
returns to* SIR ANTHONY) Faith, sir, I am so confounded,
and so – so – confused! I told you I should be so, sir, I   65
knew it. The – the – tremor of my passion entirely takes
away my presence of mind.

SIR ANTHONY

But it don't take away your voice, fool, does it? Go up
and speak to her directly!

> ABSOLUTE *makes signs to* MRS MALAPROP
> *to leave them together*

MRS MALAPROP

Sir Anthony, shall we leave them together? (*Aside to*   70
[LYDIA]) Ah, you stubborn little vixen!

SIR ANTHONY

Not yet, ma'am, not yet! (*Aside to* [ABSOLUTE])
What the devil are you at? Unlock your jaws, sirrah, or –

> ABSOLUTE *draws near* LYDIA

51, 58, 72 s.d. ed. (*Aside to him* 75, 76)
  62 *must be* 76 (is 75)
  63 s.d. ed. (*Absolute attempts* 75, 76)

ABSOLUTE

Now heaven send she may be too sullen to look round!
(*Aside*) I must disguise my voice. (*Speaks in a low hoarse* 75
tone) Will not Miss Languish lend an ear to the mild
accents of true love? Will not –

SIR ANTHONY

What the devil ails the fellow? Why don't you speak out,
not stand croaking like a frog in a quinsy!

ABSOLUTE

The – the – excess of my awe, and my – my – my 80
modesty, quite choke me!

SIR ANTHONY

Ah, your *modesty* again! I'll tell you what, Jack. If you
don't speak out directly, and glibly too, I shall be in such
a rage! Mrs Malaprop, I wish the lady would favour us
with something more than a side-front! 85

MRS MALAPROP *seems to chide* LYDIA

ABSOLUTE

So! All will out I see! (*Goes up to* LYDIA, *speaks softly*)
Be not surprised, my Lydia: suppress all surprise at
present.

LYDIA

(*Aside*) Heavens! 'Tis Beverley's voice! Sure he can't
have imposed on Sir Anthony too! (*Looks round by* 90
degrees, then starts up) Is this possible? My Beverley!
How can this be? My Beverley?

ABSOLUTE

(*Aside*) Ah! 'Tis all over.

SIR ANTHONY

Beverley! The devil. Beverley! What can the girl mean?
This is my son, Jack Absolute! 95

MRS MALAPROP

For shame, hussy, for shame! Your head runs so on that
fellow, that you have him always in your eyes! Beg
Captain Absolute's pardon directly.

LYDIA

I see no Captain Absolute, but my loved Beverley!

79 *frog in a quinsy* frog with a sore throat
85 *side-front* side view, profile

SIR ANTHONY

Zounds, the girl's mad! Her brain's turned by reading!   100

MRS MALAPROP

O' my conscience, I believe so! What do you mean by
Beverley, hussy? You saw Captain Absolute before today;
there he is: your husband that shall be.

LYDIA

With all my soul, ma'am. When I refuse my Beverley –

SIR ANTHONY

O, she's as mad as Bedlam! Or has this fellow been   105
playing us a rogue's trick? Come here, sirrah! Who the
devil are you?

ABSOLUTE

Faith, sir, I am not quite clear myself; but I'll endeavour
to recollect.

SIR ANTHONY

Are you my son, or not? Answer for your mother, you   110
dog, if you won't for me.

MRS MALAPROP

Ay, sir, who are you? O mercy! I begin to suspect!

ABSOLUTE

(Aside) Ye powers of impudence befriend me! [To SIR ANTHONY]
Sir Anthony, most assuredly I am your wife's son;
and that I sincerely believe myself to be *yours* also, I   115
hope my duty has always shown. [To MRS MALAPROP]
Mrs Malaprop, I am your most respectful admirer, and
shall be proud to add *affectionate nephew*. [To LYDIA]
I need not tell my Lydia that she sees her faithful
Beverley, who, knowing the singular generosity of her   120
temper, assumed that name, and a station, which has proved
a test of the most disinterested love, which he now hopes
to enjoy in a more elevated character.

LYDIA

(*Sullenly*) So! There will be no elopement after all!

---

105 *Bedlam* a hospital in London (full name, 'The Hospital of St Mary of Bethlehem') that
     was an asylum for lunatics
110 *for your mother* to preserve your mother's good name
121 *station* rank
122 *disinterested* unbiased (by financial considerations)
123 *in a more* 76 (in a a more 75)
     more elevated character elevated by rank, elevated by marriage

SIR ANTHONY

Upon my soul, Jack, thou art a very impudent fellow! To 125
do you justice, I think I never saw a piece of more
consummate assurance!

ABSOLUTE

O, you flatter me, sir; you compliment. 'Tis my *modesty*,
you know, sir, my *modesty* that has stood in my way.

SIR ANTHONY

Well, I am glad you are not the dull, insensible varlet you 130
pretended to be, however! I'm glad you have made a fool
of your father, you dog; I am. So this was your *penitence*,
your *duty*, and *obedience*! I thought it was damned
sudden! You 'never heard their names before', not you!
'What, the Languishes of Worcestershire', hey? 'If you 135
could please me in the affair, 'twas all you desired!' Ah!
You dissembling villain! What! (*Pointing to* LYDIA)
'She squints, don't she? A little red-haired girl', hey?
Why, you hypocritical young rascal, I wonder you a'n't
ashamed to hold up your head! 140

ABSOLUTE

'Tis with difficulty, sir. I *am* confused, very much
confused, as you must perceive.

MRS MALAPROP

O lud! Sir Anthony! A new light breaks in upon me! Hey!
How! What! Captain, did *you* write the letters then? What!
Am I to thank *you* for the elegant compilation of 'an old 145
weather-beaten she-dragon', hey? O mercy! Was it *you*
that reflected on my parts of speech?

ABSOLUTE

Dear sir, my modesty will be overpowered at last, if you
don't assist me. I shall certainly not be able to stand it!

SIR ANTHONY

Come, come, Mrs Malaprop. We must forget and forgive. 150
Od's life, matters have taken so clever a turn all of a
sudden, that I could find in my heart to be so good
humoured, and so gallant! Hey, Mrs Malaprop!

---

130 *varlet* rogue, scoundrel
135 *the Languishes* 76 (Languishes 75)
145 *Am I* 76 (I am 75)
      compilation for, appellation
151 *clever* agreeable

MRS MALAPROP

Well, Sir Anthony, since *you* desire it, we will not
anticipate the past. So mind, young people. Our   155
retrospection will now be all to the future.

SIR ANTHONY

Come, we must leave them together. Mrs Malaprop, they
long to fly into each other's arms, I warrant! Jack isn't the
cheek as I said, hey? And the eye, you rogue! And the lip,
hey? Come, Mrs Malaprop, we'll not disturb their   160
tenderness: theirs is the time of life for happiness!
(*Sings*) 'Youth's the season made for joy', hey! Od's life!
I'm in such spirits, I don't know what I couldn't do!
Permit me, ma'am. (*Gives his hand to* MRS MALAPROP.
Sings) 'Tol-de-rol'. Gad I should like a little fooling   165
myself. [*Sings*] 'Tol-de-rol! De-rol!'

Exit singing, and handing MRS MALAPROP

LYDIA *sits sullenly in her chair*

ABSOLUTE

(*Aside*) So much thought bodes me no good. [*To* LYDIA]
So grave, Lydia!

LYDIA

Sir!

ABSOLUTE

(*Aside*) So! Egad! I thought as much! That damned   170
monosyllable has froze me! [*To* LYDIA] What, Lydia,
now that we are as happy in our *friends' consent*, as in
our *mutual vows* –

LYDIA

(*Peevishly*) *Friends' consent*, indeed!

---

155 *anticipate* foresee; for, exacerbate
156 *retrospection* recall; for, introspection
159 *rogue* 76 (dog 75)
162 '*Youth's the season made for joy*' The song sung by Macheath and his whores in John Gay's
      The Beggar's Opera (1728), II.iv: 'Youth's the season made for joys, / Love is then our
      duty . . .'
169 *Sir!* A rebuke for calling Lydia by her first name – a familiarity allowed to 'Beverley' but
      not Absolute

ABSOLUTE

Come, come, we must lay aside some of our romance. A 175
little *wealth* and *comfort* may be endured after all. And, for
your fortune, the lawyers shall make such settlements as –

LYDIA

Lawyers! I *hate* lawyers!

ABSOLUTE

Nay then, we will not wait for their lingering forms, but
instantly procure the licence, and – 180

LYDIA

The *licence*! I *hate* licence!

ABSOLUTE

O my love! *Be* not so unkind! (*Kneeling*) Thus let me
entreat.

LYDIA

Pshaw! What signifies kneeling, when you know I *must*
have you? 185

ABSOLUTE

(*Rising*) Nay, madam, there shall be no constraint upon
your inclinations, I promise you. If I have lost your *heart*,
I resign the rest. (*Aside*) Gad, I must try what a little *spirit*
will do.

LYDIA

(*Rising*) Then, sir, let me tell you, the interest you had 190
there was acquired by a mean, unmanly imposition, and
deserves the punishment of fraud. What, you have been
treating *me* like a *child*, humouring my romance, and
laughing, I suppose, at your success!

ABSOLUTE

You wrong me, Lydia, you wrong me. Only hear – 195

LYDIA

(*Walking about in heat*) So, while *I* fondly imagined we
were deceiving my relations, and flattered myself that I
should outwit and incense them *all* – behold! My hopes
are to be crushed at once by my aunt's consent and

---

177 *settlements* legal arrangements. Jack offers to have legal documents so drawn up that
Lydia keeps control of her fortune.
180 *licence* marriage licence
196 *fondly* foolishly

approbation! And *I* am *myself*, the only dupe at last!   200
(*Taking a miniature from her bosom*) But here, sir, here
is the picture – Beverley's picture – which I have worn,
night and day, in spite of threats and entreaties! There, sir,
(*Flings it to him*) and be assured I throw the original from
my heart as easily!   205

ABSOLUTE

Nay, nay, ma'am, we will not differ as to that. Here,
(*Taking out a picture*) *here* is Miss Lydia Languish. What
a difference! Ay, *there* is the heavenly assenting smile
that first gave soul and spirit to my hopes! Those are the
lips which sealed a vow, as yet scarce dry in Cupid's   210
calendar! And *there* the *half* resentful blush, that *would*
have checked the ardour of my thanks. Well, all that's
past! All over indeed! There, madam. In *beauty*, that copy
is not equal to you, but in my mind its merit over the
original, in being still the same, is such – that – I cannot   215
find in my heart to *part with* it. (*Puts it up again*)

LYDIA

(*Softening*) 'Tis *your own* doing, sir. I, I, I suppose you
are perfectly satisfied.

ABSOLUTE

O, most certainly. Sure, now, this is much better than
being in love! Ha, ha, ha! There's some spirit in *this*!   220
What signifies breaking some scores of solemn promises –
all that's of no consequence, you know. To be sure,
people will say that Miss didn't know her own mind, but
never mind that. Or perhaps they may be ill-natured
enough to hint that the gentleman grew tired of the lady   225
and forsook her – but don't let that fret you.

LYDIA

There's no bearing his insolence.   (*Bursts into tears*)

---

200 *at last* 76 (75 continues: ABSOLUTE Nay, but hear me – LYDIA No, sir, you could not think
that such paltry artifices could please me when the mask was thrown off! But I suppose,
since your tricks have made you secure of my *fortune*, you are little solicitous about my
affections.)

221 *promises* 76 (75 continues: half an hundred vows, under one's hand, with the marks of a
dozen or two angels to witness)

Enter MRS MALAPROP *and* SIR ANTHONY ABSOLUTE

MRS MALAPROP
(*Entering*) Come, we must interrupt your billing and
cooing a while.

LYDIA
(*Sobbing*) *This* is *worse* than your treachery and deceit,   230
you base ingrate!

SIR ANTHONY
What the devil's the matter now! Zounds, Mrs Malaprop,
this is the *oddest billing* and *cooing* I ever heard! But
what the deuce is the meaning of it? I'm quite astonished!

ABSOLUTE
Ask the lady, sir.   235

MRS MALAPROP
O mercy! I'm quite analysed for my part! Why, Lydia,
what is the reason of this?

LYDIA
Ask the *gentleman*, ma'am.

SIR ANTHONY
Zounds, I shall be in a frenzy! Why, Jack, you are not
come out to be anyone else, are you?   240

MRS MALAPROP
Ay, sir, there's no more *trick*, is there? You are not like
Cerberus, *three* gentlemen at once, are you?

ABSOLUTE
You'll not let me speak. I say the *lady* can account for *this*
much better than I can.

LYDIA
Ma'am, you once commanded me never to think of   245
Beverley again. *There* is the man. I now obey you; for,
from this moment, I renounce him for ever.   *Exit*

MRS MALAPROP
O mercy, and miracles! What a turn here is. Why sure,
Captain, you haven't behaved disrespectfully to my niece?

---

236 *analysed* for, paralyzed or amazed
239 *Jack* 76 (Jack, you scoundrel 75)
242 *Cerberus* the three-headed dog that guarded the entrance to Hades in classical
     mythology

SIR ANTHONY

Ha, ha, ha! Ha, ha, ha! Now I see it. Ha, ha, ha! Now I see   250
it. You have been too lively, Jack.

ABSOLUTE

Nay, sir, upon my word –

SIR ANTHONY

Come, no lying, Jack. I'm sure 'twas so.

MRS MALAPROP

O lud! Sir Anthony! O fie, Captain!

ABSOLUTE

Upon my soul, ma'am –   255

SIR ANTHONY

Come, no excuses, Jack. Why, your father, you rogue,
was so before you. The blood of the Absolutes was
always impatient. Ha, ha, ha! Poor little Lydia! Why,
you've frightened her, you dog, you have.

ABSOLUTE

By all that's good, sir –   260

SIR ANTHONY

Zounds, say no more, I tell you. Mrs Malaprop shall make
your peace. [To MRS MALAPROP] You must make his
peace, Mrs Malaprop; you must tell her 'tis Jack's way.
Tell her 'tis all our ways; it runs in the blood of our family!
Come, get away, Jack. Ha, ha, ha! Mrs Malaprop, a young   265
villain!

(Push[es] [ABSOLUTE] out)

MRS MALAPROP

O, Sir Anthony! O fie, Captain!

Exeunt severally

265   *get away* 76 (get on 75)

[Act IV,] Scene iii

The North Parade

Enter SIR LUCIUS O'TRIGGER

SIR LUCIUS

I wonder where this Captain Absolute hides himself. Upon
my conscience, these officers are always in one's way in
love-affairs. I remember I might have married Lady
Dorothy Carmine, if it had not been for a little rogue of
a major, who ran away with her before she could get a   5
sight of me! And I wonder, too, what it is the ladies can
see in them to be so fond of them – unless it be a touch of
the old serpent in 'em, that makes the little creatures be
caught, like vipers with a bit of red cloth. Ha, isn't this
the Captain coming? Faith, it is! There is a probability of   10
succeeding about that fellow that is mighty provoking!
Who the devil is he talking to?   (*Steps aside*)

Enter [JACK] ABSOLUTE

ABSOLUTE

To what fine purpose I have been plotting! A noble reward
for all my schemes, upon my soul! A little gypsy! I did not
think her romance could have made her so damned absurd   15
either. 'Sdeath, I never was in a worse humour in my life!
I could cut my own throat, or any other person's, with the
greatest pleasure in the world!

SIR LUCIUS

[*Aside*] O, faith! I'm in the luck of it. I never could have
found him in a sweeter temper for my purpose. To be sure,   20
I'm just come in the nick! Now to enter into conversation
with him, and so quarrel genteelly. (*Goes up to*
ABSOLUTE) With regard to that matter, Captain, I must
beg leave to differ in opinion with you.

Scene [iii] (scene iv 75, 76)

8 *the old serpent* the devil

9 *red cloth* women are attracted by 'redcoats' – the uniform worn by soldiers – in the same
   way that vipers were thought to be attracted by red cloth

14 *gypsy* changeable woman, cheat

ABSOLUTE

Upon my word then, you must be a very subtle disputant, 25
because, sir, I happened just then to be giving no opinion
at all.

SIR LUCIUS

That's no reason. For give me leave to tell you, a man may
think an untruth as well as *speak* one.

ABSOLUTE

Very true, sir, but if the man never utters his thoughts, I 30
should think they *might* stand a *chance* of escaping
controversy.

SIR LUCIUS

Then, sir, you differ in opinion with me, which amounts
to the same thing.

ABSOLUTE

Hark'ee, Sir Lucius, if I had not before known you to be 35
a gentleman, upon my soul, I should not have discovered
it at this interview: for what you can drive at, unless you
mean to quarrel with me, I cannot conceive!

SIR LUCIUS

I humbly thank you, sir, for the quickness of your
apprehension; (*Bowing*) you have named the very thing I 40
would be at.

ABSOLUTE

Very well, sir, I shall certainly not baulk your inclinations;
but I should be glad you would please to explain your
motives.

SIR LUCIUS

Pray, sir, be easy. The quarrel is a very pretty quarrel as it 45
stands; we should only spoil it by trying to explain it.
However, your memory is very short, or you could not
have forgot an affront you passed on me within this week.
So no more, but name your time and place.

ABSOLUTE

Well, sir, since you are so bent on it, the sooner the 50
better. Let it be this evening here, by the Spring Gardens.
We shall scarcely be interrupted.

42   *baulk* disappoint, frustrate
49   *name your time and place* the person who received a challenge had a right to chose time
     and place for the duel itself

[138]

SIR LUCIUS

Faith! That same interruption in affairs of this nature
shows very great ill-breeding. I don't know what's the
reason, but in England, if a thing of this kind gets wind,   55
people make such a pother, that a gentleman can never
fight in peace and quietness. However, if it's the same to
you, Captain, I should take it as a particular kindness, if
you'd let us meet in Kingsmead Fields, as a little
business will call me there about six o'clock, and I may   60
dispatch both matters at once.

ABSOLUTE

'Tis the same to me exactly. A little after six, then, we will
discuss this matter more seriously.

SIR LUCIUS

If you please, sir. There will be very pretty small-sword
light, though it won't do for a long shot. So that matter's   65
settled, and my mind's at ease.   *Exit*

Enter FAULKLAND, *meeting* ABSOLUTE

ABSOLUTE

Well met. I was going to look for you. O, Faulkland! All
the demons of spite and disappointment have conspired
against me! I'm so vexed, that if I had not the prospect of
a resource in being knocked o' the head by and bye, I   70
should scarce have spirits to tell you the cause.

FAULKLAND

What can you mean? Has Lydia changed her mind? I
should have thought her duty and inclination would now
have pointed to the same object.

---

51   *Spring Gardens* described in *The New Bath Guide* (1771) as 'a public garden, . . . very pleas-
ingly and judiciously laid out . . . for the summer amusement and recreation of the
inhabitants and company in this city, who are allowed to walk here the whole season on
paying a subscription of half a crown'. It lay just over the river from the Grove on the
Bathwick side of Pulteney Bridge.

52   *We shall scarcely be* We are unlikely to be

55   *gets wind* becomes known

59–60 *little business* the duel Sir Lucius has arranged between 'Beverley' and Bob Acres

64–5 *small-sword light* enough light to fight with a fencing-sword (it will not be light enough
for a duel with pistols)

70   *resource* entertainment

ABSOLUTE

Ay, just as the eyes do of a person who squints. When her   75
love-eye was fixed on *me*, t'other, her *eye* of *duty*, was
finely obliqued. But when duty bid her point *that* the same
way, off t'other turned on a swivel and secured its retreat
with a frown!

FAULKLAND

But what's the resource you –   80

ABSOLUTE

O, to wind up the whole, a good-natured Irishman here
has (*Mimicking* SIR LUCIUS) 'begged leave to have the
pleasure' of cutting my throat, and I mean to indulge him.
That's all.

FAULKLAND

Prithee, be serious.   85

ABSOLUTE

'Tis fact, upon my soul. Sir Lucius O'Trigger – you know
him by sight – for some affront, which I am sure I never
intended, has obliged me to meet him this evening at six
o'clock; 'tis on that account I wished to see you. You must
go with me.   90

FAULKLAND

Nay, there must be some mistake, sure. Sir Lucius shall
explain himself, and I dare say matters may be
accommodated. But this evening, did you say? I wish it
had been any other time.

ABSOLUTE

Why? There will be light enough. There will, as Sir Lucius   95
says, 'be very pretty small-sword light, though it won't do
for a long shot'. Confound his long shots!

FAULKLAND

But I am myself a good deal ruffled by a difference I
have had with Julia. My vile tormenting temper has made
me treat her so cruelly that I shall not be myself till we   100
are reconciled.

77 *obliqued* turned askew
78 *swivel . . . retreat* Jack's army background is clear here; he is describing Lydia's withdrawal
    in terms of the workings of a pivoted rest for a gun.
90 *go with me* Jack asks Faulkland to second him in the duel
93 *accommodated* resolved, put right

ABSOLUTE

By heavens, Faulkland, you don't deserve her.

Enter SERVANT, *gives* FAULKLAND *a letter [and exits]*

FAULKLAND

O Jack! This is from Julia. I dread to open it: I fear it may
be to take a last leave, perhaps to bid me return her letters
and restore – O! How I suffer for my folly!   105

ABSOLUTE

Here, let me see. (*Takes the letter and opens it*) Ay, a final
sentence indeed! 'Tis all over with you, faith!

FAULKLAND

Nay, Jack, don't keep me in suspense.

ABSOLUTE

Hear then. 'As I am convinced that my dear Faulkland's
own reflections have already upbraided him for his last   110
unkindness to me, I will not add a word on the subject. I
wish to speak with you as soon as possible. Yours ever
and truly, Julia.' There's stubbornness and resentment
for you! (*Gives [*FAULKLAND*] the letter*) Why, man,
you don't seem one whit the happier at this.   115

FAULKLAND

O, yes, I am; but – but –

ABSOLUTE

Confound your *buts*. You never hear anything that would
make another man bless himself, but you immediately
damn it with a *but*.

FAULKLAND

Now, Jack, as you are my friend, own honestly: don't you   120
think there is something forward, something indelicate in
this haste to forgive? Women should never sue for
reconciliation: *that* should *always* come from us. *They*
should retain their coldness till *wooed* to kindness, and
their *pardon*, like their *love*, should 'not unsought be won.'   125

---

125 '*not unsought be won*' A quotation from John Milton's *Paradise Lost* (1667), 8, 500–7,
where Adam describes his first meeting with Eve: 'She heard me thus, and . . . innocence
and virgin modesty, / Her virtue and the conscience of her worth, / That would be wooed,
and not unsought be won, / Not obvious, not obtrusive, but retired . . . / Wrought in her
so, that, seeing me, she turned'.

ABSOLUTE

I have not patience to listen to you: thou'rt incorrigible!
So say no more on the subject. I must go to settle a few
matters. Let me see you before six, remember, at my
lodgings. A poor industrious devil like me, who have
toiled and drudged and plotted to gain my ends, and am   130
at last disappointed by other people's folly, may in pity be
allowed to swear and grumble a little; but a captious
sceptic in love, a slave to fretfulness and whim, who has
no difficulties but of *his own* creating, is a subject more
fit for ridicule than compassion!   *Exit*   135

FAULKLAND

I feel his reproaches! Yet I would not change this too
exquisite nicety for the gross content with which *he*
tramples on the thorns of love. His engaging me in this
duel has started an idea in my head, which I will instantly
pursue. I'll use it as the touchstone of Julia's sincerity   140
and disinterestedness. If her love prove pure and sterling
ore, my name will rest on it with honour! And once I've
stamped it there, I lay aside my doubts forever. But if the
dross of selfishness, the allay of pride, predominate, 'twill
be best to leave her as a toy for some less cautious fool to   145
sigh for.   *Exit*

---

137   *nicety* sensitivity
140   *touchstone* black stone against which gold and silver were tested for purity
141   *disinterestedness* selflessness
141–6 *If her love . . . sigh for* Julia's love is compared to a coin: 'good' metal will be worthy of
       Faulkland's name (just as 'good' money bears the king's name); 'bad' metal is to be left
       for 'some less cautious fool'.
144   *dross* scum thrown away from melting metals
145   *toy* trifling, inconsequential person

Act V, Scene i

JULIA [MELVILLE]*'s dressing-room*

JULIA [*alone*]

JULIA

How this message has alarmed me! What dreadful accident
can he mean! Why such charge to be alone? O Faulkland!
How many unhappy moments, how many tears have you
cost me!

Enter FAULKLAND, *muffled up in a riding-coat*

What means this? Why this caution, Faulkland?   5

FAULKLAND

Alas, Julia, I am come to take a long farewell.

JULIA

Heavens! What do you mean?

FAULKLAND

You see before you a wretch, whose life is forfeited. Nay,
start not! The infirmity of my temper has drawn all this
misery on me. I left you fretful and passionate. An   10
untoward accident drew me into a quarrel. The event is,
that I must fly this kingdom instantly. O Julia, had I been
so fortunate as to have called you mine entirely, before
this mischance had fallen on me, I should not so deeply
dread my banishment!   15

JULIA

My soul is oppressed with sorrow at the *nature* of your
misfortune. Had these adverse circumstances arisen from

---

0   s.d 1 ed. (*Julia sola* 75, 76)

2   *charge* order

6   *a long farewell* The phrase is from Shakespeare, *Henry VIII*, III.ii.352: 'A long farewell, to
    all my greatness! / This is the state of man: to-day he puts forth / The tender leaves of
    hopes; to-morrow blossoms, / And bears his blushing honours thick upon him; / The
    third day comes a frost, a killing frost . . .'

8   *life is forfeited* Faulkland pretends he has done something – probably killed someone in
    a duel – for which he must pay with his life.

11 *event* consequence

15 *banishment!* 76 (75 continues: But no more of that: your heart and promise were given
    to one happy in friends, character, and station! They are not bound to wait upon a
    solitary, guilty exile.)

a less fatal cause, I should have felt strong comfort in the
thought that I could *now* chase from your bosom every
doubt of the warm sincerity of my love. My heart has long   20
known no other guardian. I now entrust my person to your
honour: we will fly together. When safe from pursuit, my
father's will may be fulfilled, and I receive a legal claim to
be the partner of your sorrows and tenderest comforter.
Then, on the bosom of your wedded Julia, you may lull   25
your keen regret to slumbering; while virtuous love, with
a cherub's hand, shall smooth the brow of upbraiding
thought and pluck the thorn from compunction.

FAULKLAND

O Julia! I am bankrupt in gratitude! But the time is so
pressing, it calls on you for so hasty a resolution. Would   30
you not wish some hours to weigh the advantages you
forego, and what little compensation poor Faulkland can
make you beside his solitary love?

JULIA

I ask not a moment. No, Faulkland, I have loved you for
yourself; and if I now, more than ever, prize the solemn   35
engagement which so long has pledged us to each other,
it is because it leaves no room for hard aspersions on my
fame, and puts the seal of duty to an act of love. But let
us not linger. Perhaps this delay –

FAULKLAND

'Twill be better I should not venture out again till dark.   40
Yet am I grieved to think what numberless distresses will
press heavy on your gentle disposition!

JULIA

Perhaps your fortune may be forfeited by this unhappy act.
I know not whether 'tis so, but sure that alone can never
make us unhappy. The little I have will be sufficient to   45
support us; and *exile* never should be splendid.

FAULKLAND

Ay, but in such an abject state of life, my wounded pride
perhaps may increase the natural fretfulness of my

27 *upbraiding* chiding, reproaching
28 *compunction* conscience
29 *bankrupt* without any means of repaying. Faulkland returns to a monetary metaphor,
    see IV.iii.141–6.

temper, till I become a rude, morose companion, beyond
your patience to endure. Perhaps the recollection of a   50
deed my conscience cannot justify may haunt me in such
gloomy and unsocial fits that I shall hate the tenderness
that would relieve me, break from your arms, and quarrel
with your fondness!

JULIA

If your thoughts should assume so unhappy a bent, you   55
will the more want some mild and affectionate spirit to
watch over and console you: one who, by bearing *your*
infirmities with gentleness and resignation, may teach
you *so* to bear the evils of your fortune.

FAULKLAND

Julia, I have proved you to the quick, and with this   60
useless device I throw away all my doubts. How shall I
plead to be forgiven this last unworthy effect of my
restless, unsatisfied disposition?

JULIA

Has no such disaster happened as you related?

FAULKLAND

I am ashamed to own that it was all pretended. Yet in pity,   65
Julia, do not kill me with resenting a fault which never
can be repeated. But, sealing, this once, my pardon, let me
tomorrow, in the face of heaven, receive my future guide
and monitress, and expiate my past folly by years of
tender adoration.   70

JULIA

Hold, Faulkland! That you are free from a crime which I
before feared to name, heaven knows how sincerely I
rejoice! These are tears of thankfulness for that! But that
your cruel doubts should have urged you to an imposition
that has wrung my heart gives me now a pang more   75
keen than I can express!

49   *rude* ungentle
60   *Julia* 76 (O Julia 75)
     proved you to the quick tested you to the limit
61   *useless device* redundant pretence
69   *monitress* female advisor
74   *imposition* trick, deception

FAULKLAND

By heavens! Julia –

JULIA

Yet hear me. My father loved you, Faulkland, and you
preserved the life that tender parent gave me. In his
presence I pledged my hand – *joyfully* pledged it – where   80
before I had given my heart. When, soon after, I lost that
parent, it seemed to me that providence had, in Faulkland,
shown me whither to transfer, without a pause, my
grateful duty, as well as my affection. Hence I have been
content to bear from you what pride and delicacy would   85
have forbid me from another. I will not upbraid you by
repeating how you have trifled with my sincerity.

FAULKLAND

I confess it all! Yet hear –

JULIA

After such a year of trial, I might have flattered myself
that I should not have been insulted with a new probation   90
of my sincerity, as cruel as unnecessary! I now see it is not
in your nature to be content, or confident, in love. With this
conviction, I never will be yours. While I had hopes that
my persevering attention and unreproaching kindness
might in time reform your temper, I should have been   95
happy to have gained a dearer influence over you; but I
will not furnish you with a licensed power to keep alive an
incorrigible fault, at the expense of one who never would
contend with you.

FAULKLAND

Nay, but Julia, by my soul and honour, if after this –   100

JULIA

But one word more. As my faith has once been given to
you, I never will barter it with another. I shall pray for
your happiness with the truest sincerity; and the dearest
blessing I can ask of heaven to send you will be to charm
you from that unhappy temper, which alone has prevented   105

82 *providence* divine direction

91 *unnecessary!* 76 (75 continues: A trick of such a nature as to show me plainly, that when
I thought you loved me best, you even then regarded me as a mean dissembler; an
artful, prudent hypocrite. FAULKLAND Never! Never!)

97 *licensed power* allowable power; the reference is to the marriage license and the rights he
would have on acquiring it

the performance of our solemn engagement. All I request
of *you* is that you will yourself reflect upon this infirmity,
and when you number up the many true delights it has
deprived you of, let it not be your *least* regret, that it lost
you the love of one who would have followed you in   110
beggary through the world!   *Exit*

FAULKLAND

She's gone! Forever! There was an awful resolution in
her manner that riveted me to my place. O fool! Dolt!
Barbarian! Cursed as I am with more imperfections than
my fellow-wretches, kind fortune sent a heaven-gifted   115
cherub to my aid, and, like a ruffian, I have driven her
from my side! I must now haste to my appointment. Well,
my mind is tuned for such a scene. I shall wish only to
become a principal in it, and reverse the tale my cursed
folly put me upon forging here. O love! Tormentor!   120
Fiend! – whose influence, like the moon's, acting on men
of dull souls, makes idiots of them, but meeting subtler
spirits, betrays their course and urges sensibility to
madness!   *Exit*

Enter MAID *and* LYDIA [LANGUISH]

MAID

My mistress, ma'am, I know, was here just now. Perhaps   125
she is only in the next room.   *Exit*

LYDIA

Heigh-ho! Though he has used me so, this fellow runs
strangely in my head. I believe one lecture from my grave
cousin will make me recall him.

Enter JULIA [MELVILLE]

O Julia, I am come to you with such an appetite for   130
consolation. Lud, child, what's the matter with you?
You have been crying! I'll be hanged if that Faulkland
has not been tormenting you!

---

119   *a principal* a participant
121   *like the moon's* Madness was thought to be caused by the influence of the moon – hence
        the term 'lunacy' (from *luna*, moon).
122   *subtler* more sensitive

JULIA

You mistake the cause of my uneasiness. Something *has* flurried me a little. Nothing that you can guess at. (*Aside*)   135
I would not accuse Faulkland to a sister!

LYDIA

Ah, whatever vexations you may have, I can assure you mine surpass them. You know who Beverley proves to be?

JULIA

I will now own to you, Lydia, that Mr Faulkland had before informed me of the whole affair. Had young   140
Absolute been the person you took him for, I should not have accepted your confidence on the subject without a serious endeavour to counteract your caprice.

LYDIA

So, then, I see I have been deceived by every one! But I don't care; I'll never have him.   145

JULIA

Nay, Lydia –

LYDIA

Why, is it not provoking, when I thought we were coming to the prettiest distress imaginable, to find myself made a mere Smithfield bargain of at last? There had I projected one of the most sentimental elopements! So becoming a   150
disguise! So amiable a ladder of ropes! Conscious moon, four horses, Scotch parson; with such surprise to Mrs Malaprop, and such paragraphs in the newspapers! O, I shall die with disappointment.

JULIA

I don't wonder at it!   155

LYDIA

Now – sad reverse! What have I to expect, but, after a deal of flimsy preparation, with a bishop's licence, and my

---

149 *Smithfield bargain* monetary transaction in which the buyer is fooled. Smithfield was the central meat market in London famous for its sharp practices.

151 *Conscious* Sympathetic

152 *Scotch parson* In England only people over the age of 21 were allowed to marry without their parents' consent; Scotland, which had no such rules, was famously the place to which young people ran away when they eloped. The parson is probably Joseph Paisley, famous for officiating at runaway marriages.

157 *bishop's licence* gave permission to marry in the church of a parish in which one of the couple resides

aunt's blessing, to go simpering up to the altar, or
perhaps be cried three times in a country church, and
have an unmannerly fat clerk ask the consent of every   160
butcher in the parish to join John Absolute and Lydia
Languish, *spinster*! O, that I should live to hear myself
called spinster!

JULIA

Melancholy, indeed!

LYDIA

How mortifying to remember the dear delicious shifts I   165
used to be put to, to gain half a minute's conversation
with this fellow! How often have I stole forth, in the
coldest night in January, and found him in the garden,
stuck like a dripping statue! There would he kneel to me
in the snow, and sneeze and cough so pathetically! He   170
shivering with cold, and I with apprehension! And while
the freezing blast numbed our joints, how warmly would
he press me to pity his flame, and glow with mutual
ardour! Ah, Julia! That was something like being in love.

JULIA

If I were in spirits, Lydia, I should chide you only by   175
laughing heartily at you. But it suits more the situation
of my mind, at present, earnestly to entreat you not to
let a man, who loves you with sincerity, suffer that
unhappiness from your *caprice*, which I know too well
caprice can inflict.   180

LYDIA

O lud! What has brought my aunt here?

Enter MRS MALAPROP, FAG, *and* DAVID

MRS MALAPROP

So! So! Here's fine work! Here's fine suicide, parricide,
and simulation going on in the fields, and Sir Anthony
not to be found to prevent the antistrophe!

---

159 *cried three times* the alternative to procuring a bishop's licence was to have the marriage
     banns read on three successive Sundays in the church in which the marriage was to take
     place
165 *shifts* tricks, stratagems
182 *parricide* the murdering of relatives; for, homicide
183 *simulation* 76 (salivation 75), for, dissimulation
184 *antistrophe* one of the divisions of the Greek choral ode; for, catastrophe

JULIA

For heaven's sake, madam, what's the meaning of this?   185

MRS MALAPROP

That gentleman can tell you: 'twas he enveloped the affair
to me.

LYDIA

(*To* FAG) Do, sir, will you inform us?

FAG

Ma'am, I should hold myself very deficient in every
requisite that forms the man of breeding, if I delayed a   190
moment to give all the information in my power to a
lady so deeply interested in the affair as you are.

LYDIA

But quick! Quick, sir!

FAG

True, ma'am, as you say, one should be quick in
divulging matters of this nature; for should we be tedious,   195
perhaps while we are flourishing on the subject, two or
three lives may be lost!

LYDIA

O patience! [*To* MRS MALAPROP] Do, ma'am, for
heaven's sake, tell us what is the matter?

MRS MALAPROP

Why, murder's the matter! Slaughter's the matter!   200
Killing's the matter! But he can tell you the
perpendiculars.

LYDIA

Then, prithee, sir, be brief.

FAG

Why then, ma'am, as to murder, I cannot take upon me to
say; and as to slaughter, or manslaughter, that will be as   205
the jury finds it.

LYDIA

But who, sir – who are engaged in this?

FAG

Faith, ma'am, one is a young gentleman whom I should
be very sorry anything was to happen to: a very pretty-

186 *enveloped* for, developed (revealed)
192 *interested in* involved in, concerned in
196 *flourishing* making rhetorical elaborations
202 *perpendiculars* for, particulars

behaved gentleman! We have lived much together, and   210
always on terms.

LYDIA

But who is this? Who? Who? Who?

FAG

My master, ma'am, my master; I speak of my master.

LYDIA

Heavens! What, Captain Absolute?

MRS MALAPROP

O, to be sure, you are frightened now!   215

JULIA

But who are with him, sir?

FAG

As to the rest, ma'am, his gentleman can inform you
better than I.

JULIA

(*To* DAVID) Do speak, friend.

DAVID

Look'ee, my lady, by the mass, there's mischief going   220
on. Folks don't use to meet for amusement with
firearms, firelocks, fire-engines, fire-screens, fire-office,
and the devil knows what other crackers besides! This,
my lady, I say, has an angry favour.

JULIA

But who is there beside Captain Absolute, friend?   225

DAVID

My poor master – under favour, for mentioning him first.
You know me, my lady, I am David, and my master, of
course, is, or *was*, Squire Acres. Then comes Squire
Faulkland.

JULIA

[*To* MRS MALAPROP] Do, ma'am, let us instantly   230
endeavour to prevent mischief.

---

211 *on terms* (1) in a friendly fashion; (2) on certain conditions – namely that Absolute pays
      Fag's wages
222–3 *firearms . . . crackers besides!* David lists everything connected to fire (rather than firearms)
      that he can come up with: firelocks are muskets, fire-engines pump jets of water, fire-
      screens are put in front of fires to shield people from the heat, fire-office is an office that
      deals with fire insurance, crackers are fireworks.
223 *besides* 75 (beside 76)
224 *favour* face

MRS MALAPROP

O fie, it would be very inelegant in us. We should only
participate things.

DAVID

Ah, do, Mrs Aunt, save a few lives. They are desperately
given, believe me. Above all, there is that bloodthirsty   235
Philistine, Sir Lucius O'Trigger.

MRS MALAPROP

Sir Lucius O'Trigger! O mercy! Have they drawn poor
little dear Sir Lucius into the scrape? Why, how, how you
stand, girl! You have no more feeling than one of the
Derbyshire putrefactions!   240

LYDIA

What are we to do, madam?

MRS MALAPROP

Why, fly with the utmost felicity, to be sure, to prevent
mischief. Here, friend – you can show us the place?

FAG

If you please, ma'am, I will conduct you. David, do you
look for Sir Anthony.   245

Exit DAVID

MRS MALAPROP

Come, girls! This gentleman will exhort us. Come, sir,
you're our envoy. Lead the way, and we'll precede.

FAG

Not a step before the ladies for the world!

MRS MALAPROP

You're sure you know the spot.

---

233 *participate* for, precipitate or exacerbate
234–5 *desperately given* in a desperate (i.e. killing) mood
236 *Philistine* from the Philistines in the Bible, belligerent, guided by materialism,
       disdainful of artistic values, and alien
240 *putrefactions* for, petrifactions; Derbyshire was famous for its fossils, stalactites and
       stalagmites.
242 *felicity* for, alacrity or velocity, both meaning speed
246 *exhort* for, escort
247 *envoy* messenger sent on behalf of someone else; for, convoy
       precede for, proceed

FAG

I think I can find it, ma'am; and one good thing is, we   250
shall hear the report of the pistols as we draw near, so we
can't well miss them. Never fear, ma'am, never fear.

Exeunt, he talking

[Act V,] Scene ii

South Parade

Enter [JACK] ABSOLUTE, *putting his sword
under his greatcoat*

ABSOLUTE

A sword seen in the streets of Bath would raise as great an
alarm as a mad dog. How provoking this is in Faulkland!
Never punctual! I shall be obliged to go without him at
last. O, the devil! Here's Sir Anthony! How shall I escape
him?   (*Muffles up his face, and takes a circle to go off*)   5

Enter SIR ANTHONY ABSOLUTE

SIR ANTHONY

How one may be deceived at a little distance! Only that
I see he don't know me, I could have sworn that was
Jack! Hey! Gad's life; it is! Why, Jack – what are you
afraid of? Hey! Sure I'm right. Why, Jack – Jack
Absolute!   (*Goes up to him*)   10

ABSOLUTE

Really, sir, you have the advantage of me: I don't
remember ever to have had the honour. My name is
Saunderson, at your service.

SIR ANTHONY

Sir, I beg your pardon, I took you – hey! Why, zounds, it
is! Stay. (*Looks up to his face*) So, so your humble   15

---

251   *report* resounding noise

0   s.d. 1–2 *putting . . . greatcoat* hiding his sword in his coat (because carrying swords was
forbidden in Bath – see III.iv.66 n.)
5   s.d. *takes a circle* walks round in a circle
8   *Jack* 76 (Jack, you dog! 75)

servant, Mr Saunderson! Why, you scoundrel, what tricks
are you after now?

ABSOLUTE

O, a joke, sir, a joke! I came here on purpose to look for
you, sir.

SIR ANTHONY

You did! Well, I am glad you were so lucky. But what are   20
you muffled up so for? What's this for? Hey?

ABSOLUTE

'Tis cool, sir, isn't it? Rather chilly somehow. But I shall
be late; I have a particular engagement.

SIR ANTHONY

Stay. Why, I thought you were looking for me? Pray,
Jack, where is't you are going?   25

ABSOLUTE

Going, sir?

SIR ANTHONY

Ay, where are you going?

ABSOLUTE

Where am I going?

SIR ANTHONY

You unmannerly puppy!

ABSOLUTE

I was going, sir, to – to – to – to Lydia, sir to Lydia – to   30
make matters up if I could. And I was looking for you, sir,
to – to –

SIR ANTHONY

To go with you, I suppose. Well, come along.

ABSOLUTE

O, zounds, no, sir: not for the world! I wished to meet
with you, sir, to – to – to – you find it cool, I'm sure, sir: 35
you'd better not stay out.

SIR ANTHONY

Cool? Not at all. Well, Jack, and what will you say to
Lydia?

ABSOLUTE

O, sir, beg her pardon, humour her, promise and vow. But
I detain you, sir. Consider the cold air on your gout.   40

SIR ANTHONY

O, not at all, not at all! I'm in no hurry. Ah, Jack, you
youngsters, when once you are wounded here. (*Putting his*

hand to ABSOLUTE'*s breast*) Hey! What the deuce have
you got here?

ABSOLUTE

Nothing, sir. Nothing.   45

SIR ANTHONY

What's this? Here's something damned hard!

ABSOLUTE

O, trinkets, sir! Trinkets. A bauble for Lydia!

SIR ANTHONY

Nay, let me see your taste. (*Pulls his coat open. The
sword falls*) Trinkets! A bauble for Lydia! Zounds, sirrah,
you are not going to cut her throat, are you?   50

ABSOLUTE

Ha, ha, ha! I thought it would divert you, sir, though I
didn't mean to tell you till afterwards.

SIR ANTHONY

You didn't? Yes, this is a very diverting trinket, truly.

ABSOLUTE

Sir, I'll explain to you. You know, sir, Lydia is romantic,
devilish romantic, and very absurd of course. Now, sir, I   55
intend, if she refuses to forgive me, to unsheath this sword
and swear I'll fall upon its point, and expire at her feet!

SIR ANTHONY

Fall upon fiddle-sticks' end! Why, I suppose it is the very
thing that would please her. Get along, you fool.

ABSOLUTE

Well, sir, you shall hear of my success; you shall hear.   60
'O, Lydia! forgive me, or this pointed steel –' says I.

SIR ANTHONY

'O, booby, stab away, and welcome', says she. Get along!
And damn your trinkets!

Exit ABSOLUTE

Enter DAVID, *running*

DAVID

Stop him! Stop him! Murder! Thief! Fire! Stop fire! Stop
fire! – O, Sir Anthony! Call! Call! Bid 'em stop! Murder!   65
Fire!

51 *divert* entertain, amuse

[155]

SIR ANTHONY

Fire! Murder! Where?

DAVID

Oons! He's out of sight! And I'm out of breath, for my part!
O, Sir Anthony, why didn't you stop him? Why didn't you
stop him?   70

SIR ANTHONY

Zounds! The fellow's mad! Stop whom? Stop Jack?

DAVID

Ay, the Captain, sir! There's murder and slaughter –

SIR ANTHONY

Murder!

DAVID

Ay, please you, Sir Anthony, there's all kinds of murder,
all sorts of slaughter to be seen in the fields. There's   75
fighting going on, sir, bloody sword-and-gun fighting!

SIR ANTHONY

Who are going to fight, dunce?

DAVID

Everybody that I know of, Sir Anthony. Everybody is
going to fight: my poor master, Sir Lucius O'Trigger,
your son the Captain –   80

SIR ANTHONY

O, the dog! I see his tricks. Do you know the place?

DAVID

Kingsmead Fields.

SIR ANTHONY

You know the way?

DAVID

Not an inch; but I'll call the mayor, aldermen, constables,
churchwardens and beadles. We can't be too many to   85
part them.

SIR ANTHONY

Come along, give me your shoulder! We'll get assistance
as we go – the lying villain! Well, I shall be in such a

---

74 *please you* so please you, may it be acceptable to you
84–5 *mayor . . . beadles* Fag names every civic officer he can come up with. The mayor headed
      a town or city corporation, aldermen were members of the town council, constables and
      beadles kept the peace in parishes (before the advent of the police force)
87 *shoulder* Sir Anthony is still incapacitated by gout and needs to lean on David.

frenzy. So this was the history of his trinkets! I'll bauble
him!   90

Exeunt

[Act V,] Scene iii

Kingsmead Fields

SIR LUCIUS [O'TRIGGER] *and* [BOB] ACRES, *with pistols*

ACRES

By my valour, then, Sir Lucius, forty yards is a good
distance. Od's levels and aims! I say it is a good distance.

SIR LUCIUS

Is it for muskets or small field-pieces? Upon my
conscience, Mr Acres, you must leave those things to me.
Stay now. I'll show you. (*Measures paces along the*   5
stage) There now, that is a very pretty distance; a pretty
gentleman's distance.

ACRES

Zounds! We might as well fight in a sentry-box! I tell you,
Sir Lucius, the farther he is off, the cooler I shall take
my aim.   10

SIR LUCIUS

Faith, then I suppose you would aim at him best of all if
he was out of sight!

ACRES

No, Sir Lucius, but I should think forty or eight-and-thirty
yards –

SIR LUCIUS

Foh, foh, nonsense! Three or four feet between the   15
mouths of your pistols is as good as a mile.

---

89   *his trinkets* 76 (his damned trinkets 75)

1   *forty yards* Acres and Sir Lucius are arguing as to the ideal distance to separate the two
opponents. Acres wants as wide a distance as possible, so that hitting the adversary is
unlikely: Sir Lucius wants a short distance, making killing one's opponent – or being
killed – a real possibility.
3   *muskets or small field-pieces* powerful handguns and small cannon; both carried further
than pistols
8   *sentry-box* wooden cabin large enough to hold just one soldier on sentry duty

ACRES

Od's bullets, no! By my valour, there is no merit in killing him so near: no, my dear Sir Lucius, let me bring him down at a long shot – a long shot, Sir Lucius, if you love me!   20

SIR LUCIUS

Well, the gentleman's friend and I must settle that. But tell me now, Mr Acres, in case of an accident, is there any little will or commission I could execute for you?

ACRES

I am much obliged to you, Sir Lucius, but I don't understand –   25

SIR LUCIUS

Why, you may think there's no being shot at without a little risk, and if an unlucky bullet should carry a *quietus* with it, I say it will be no time then to be bothering you about family matters.

ACRES

A *quietus*!   30

SIR LUCIUS

For instance, now, if that should be the case, would you choose to be pickled and sent home? Or would it be the same to you to lie here in the Abbey? I'm told there is very snug lying in the Abbey.

ACRES

Pickled! Snug lying in the Abbey! Od's tremors! Sir   35
Lucius, don't talk so!

SIR LUCIUS

I suppose, Mr Acres, you never were engaged in an affair of this kind before?

ACRES

No, Sir Lucius, never before.

---

18   *no* 76 (do 75)

21   *gentleman's friend and I* the two seconds

23   *execute* do – but the choice of word is unfortunate

27   *quietus* from Medieval Latin *quietus est*, 'he is quit', meaning the discharge of a debt; it came to mean a release by death after Hamlet (*Hamlet*, III.i. 84) suggested he could make his own quietus 'with a bare bodkin'.

32   *pickled* preserved in brine (a way of stopping dead bodies from decaying)

33   *lie here in the Abbey* be buried here in Bath Abbey

SIR LUCIUS

Ah! That's a pity! There's nothing like being used to a   40
thing. Pray now, how would you receive the gentleman's
shot?

ACRES

Od's files! I've practised that. (*Puts himself in an attitude*)
There, Sir Lucius, there. A side-front, hey? Od! I'll make
myself small enough: I'll stand edgeways.   45

SIR LUCIUS

Now you're quite out; for if you stand so (*Levelling at him*)
when I take my aim –

ACRES

Zounds! Sir Lucius – are you sure it is not cocked?

SIR LUCIUS

Never fear.

ACRES

But – but – you don't know; it may go off of its own head!   50

SIR LUCIUS

Foh! Be easy. Well, now if I hit you in the body, my bullet
has a double chance; for if it misses a vital part on your
right side, 'twill be very hard if it don't succeed on the left!

ACRES

A vital part!

SIR LUCIUS

But, there – fix yourself so. (*Placing him*) Let him see the   55
broad side of your full front. There – now a ball or two
may pass clean through your body, and never do any harm
at all.

ACRES

Clean through me! A ball or two clean through me!

SIR LUCIUS

Ay, may they, and it is much the genteelest attitude into   60
the bargain.

43 *files* either lines of soldiers, or swords used in fencing
    s.d *attitude* a set theatrical posture
46 *quite out* entirely wrong
50 *of its own head* of its own accord
54 *part!* 76 (75 continues: O, my poor vitals!)
57 *clean* 76 (clear 75)

ACRES

Look'ee, Sir Lucius, I'd just as lief be shot in an awkward posture as a genteel one – so, by my valour, I will stand edge-ways!

SIR LUCIUS

(*Looking at his watch*) Sure they don't mean to disappoint   65
us. Ha? No, faith, I think I see them coming.

ACRES

Hey! What? Coming?

SIR LUCIUS

Ay. Who are those yonder getting over the stile?

ACRES

There are two of them, indeed! Well, let them come, hey, Sir Lucius! We – we – we – we – won't run.   70

SIR LUCIUS

Run!

ACRES

No, I say, we *won't* run, by my valour!

SIR LUCIUS

What the devil's the matter with you?

ACRES

Nothing – nothing – my dear friend – my dear Sir Lucius – but – I – I – I don't feel quite so bold, somehow – as I   75
did.

SIR LUCIUS

O fie! Consider your honour.

ACRES

Ay – true – my honour. Do, Sir Lucius, edge in a word or two every now and then about my honour.

SIR LUCIUS

(*Looking*) Well, here they're coming.   80

ACRES

Sir Lucius, if I wa'n't with you, I should almost think I was afraid if my valour should leave me! Valour will come and go.

SIR LUCIUS

Then, pray keep it fast, while you have it.

---

62   *lief* willingly, gladly
78   *edge* 76 (hedge 75)

ACRES

Sir Lucius, I doubt it is going. Yes, my valour is certainly   85
going! It is sneaking off! I feel it oozing out, as it were, at
the palms of my hands!

SIR LUCIUS

Your honour – your honour! Here they are.

ACRES

O mercy! Now that I were safe at Clod Hall! Or could be
shot before I was aware!   90

Enter FAULKLAND *and* [JACK] ABSOLUTE

SIR LUCIUS

Gentlemen, your most obedient – ha! What, Captain Absolute!
So, I suppose, sir, you are come here, just like myself,
to do a kind office first for your friend, then to proceed
to business on your own account.

ACRES

What, Jack! My dear Jack! My dear friend!   95

ABSOLUTE

Heark'ee, Bob, Beverley's at hand.

SIR LUCIUS

Well, Mr Acres, I don't blame your saluting the gentleman
civilly. (*To* FAULKLAND) So, Mr Beverley, if you'll
choose your weapons, the Captain and I will measure
the ground.   100

FAULKLAND

My weapons, sir?

ACRES

Od's life! Sir Lucius, I'm not going to fight
Mr Faulkland; these are my particular friends.

SIR LUCIUS

What, sir, did not you come here to fight Mr Acres?

FAULKLAND

Not I, upon my word, sir.   105

---

85 *doubt* fear
89 *that* if only
98 s.d. *To* FAULKLAND Lucius, recognising everyone else, assumes that Faulkland must be
    the unknown Beverley
99–100 *measure the ground* measure out the distance to be allowed between the duellists

SIR LUCIUS

Well, now, that's mighty provoking. But I hope, Mr
Faulkland, as there are three of us come on purpose for
the game, you won't be so cantankerous as to spoil the
party by sitting out.

ABSOLUTE

O pray, Faulkland, fight to oblige Sir Lucius.   110

FAULKLAND

Nay, if Mr Acres is so bent on the matter.

ACRES

No, no, Mr Faulkland: I'll bear my disappointment like a
Christian. Look'ee, Sir Lucius, there's no occasion at all
for me to fight; and if it is the same to you, I'd as lief let
it alone.   115

SIR LUCIUS

Observe me, Mr Acres: I must not be trifled with. You
have certainly challenged somebody, and you came here
to fight him. Now, if that gentleman is willing to represent
him, I can't see, for my soul, why it isn't just the same
thing.   120

ACRES

Why, no, Sir Lucius. I tell you, 'tis one Beverley I've
challenged – a fellow, you see, that dare not show his face!
If *he* were here, I'd make him give up his pretensions
directly!

ABSOLUTE

Hold, Bob, let me set you right. There is no such man as   125
Beverley in the case. The person who assumed that name
is before you; and as his pretensions are the same in
both characters, he is ready to support them in whatever
way you please.

SIR LUCIUS

Well, this is lucky. Now you have an opportunity –   130

ACRES

What, quarrel with my dear friend Jack Absolute? Not if
he were fifty Beverleys! Zounds, Sir Lucius, you would
not have me be so unnatural.

---

111   *bent on* determined on
121   *Why, no* 76 (zounds 75)

SIR LUCIUS

Upon my conscience, Mr Acres, your valour has *oozed* away with a vengeance!   135

ACRES

Not in the least! Od's backs and abettors! I'll be your second with all my heart, and if you should get a *quietus*, you may command me entirely. I'll get you a *snug lying* in the *Abbey here*, or *pickle* you, and send you over to Blunderbuss Hall, or anything of the kind, with the   140 greatest pleasure.

SIR LUCIUS

Foh, foh! You are little better than a coward.

ACRES

Mind, gentlemen, he calls me a '*coward*'; coward was the word, by my valour!

SIR LUCIUS

Well, sir?   145

ACRES

Look'ee, Sir Lucius, 'tisn't that I mind the word coward. '*Coward*' may be said in joke. But if you had called me a *poltroon*, od's daggers and balls!

SIR LUCIUS

Well, sir?

ACRES

I should have thought you a very ill-bred man.   150

SIR LUCIUS

Foh! You are beneath my notice.

ABSOLUTE

Nay, Sir Lucius, you can't have a better second than my friend Acres. He is a most *determined dog*, called in the country, '*Fighting Bob*'. He generally *kills a man a week*, don't you, Bob?   155

ACRES

Ay, at home!

SIR LUCIUS

Well then, Captain, 'tis we must begin. So (*Draws his sword*) come out, my little counsellor, and ask the

---

136   *backs and abettors* backers (seconds in a duel) and helpers
140   *anything* 76 (any 75)
158   *counsellor* lawyer or barrister

gentleman whether he will resign the lady, without forcing
you to proceed against him?   160

ABSOLUTE

Come on then, sir; (*Draws*) since you won't let it be an
amicable suit, here's *my reply*.

Enter SIR ANTHONY ABSOLUTE, DAVID, *and*
[MRS MALAPROP, LYDIA LANGUISH, JULIA MELVILLE]

DAVID

Knock 'em all down, sweet Sir Anthony. Knock down my
master in particular, and bind his hands over to their
good behaviour!   165

SIR ANTHONY

Put up, Jack, put up, or I shall be in a frenzy. How came
you in a duel, sir?

ABSOLUTE

Faith, sir, that gentleman can tell you better than I; 'twas
he called on me, and you know, sir, I serve his majesty.

SIR ANTHONY

Here's a pretty fellow; I catch him going to cut a man's   170
throat, and he tells me he serves his majesty! Zounds,
sirrah, then how durst you draw the king's sword
against one of his subjects?

ABSOLUTE

Sir, I tell you! That gentleman called me out, without
explaining his reasons.   175

SIR ANTHONY

Gad, sir, how came you to call my son out, without
explaining your reasons?

SIR LUCIUS

Your son, sir, insulted me in a manner which my honour
could not brook.

SIR ANTHONY

Zounds! Jack, how durst you insult the gentleman in a   180

162   *amicable suit* suit settled out of court
162   s.d. ed. (*and the women* 75, 76)
164–5 *bind . . . good behaviour* a confusion of 'bind him over to his good behaviour' i.e. make
       him promise to behave; and 'bind his hands', tie him up (so that he cannot fight)
166   *Put up* Sheath your sword
169   *I serve his majesty* Absolute either says he, as an officer, must respond to the challenge;
       or that, as an officer, he would not be allowed to fight a duel.

manner which his honour could not brook?

MRS MALAPROP

Come, come, let's have no honour before ladies. Captain Absolute, come here. How could you intimidate us so? Here's Lydia has been terrified to death for you.

ABSOLUTE

For fear I should be killed, or escape, ma'am?   185

MRS MALAPROP

Nay, no delusions to the past. Lydia is convinced. Speak, child.

SIR LUCIUS

With your leave, ma'am, I must put in a word here. I believe I could interpret the young lady's silence. Now mark –   190

LYDIA

What is it you mean, sir?

SIR LUCIUS

Come, come, Delia, we must be serious now; this is no time for trifling.

LYDIA

'Tis true, sir; and your reproof bids me offer this gentleman my hand, and solicit the return of his   195 affections.

ABSOLUTE

O, my little angel, say you so? Sir Lucius, I perceive there must be some mistake here. With regard to the affront which you affirm I have given you, I can only say that it could not have been intentional. And, as you must   200 be convinced that I should not fear to support a real injury, you shall now see that I am not ashamed to atone for an inadvertency. I ask your pardon. But for this lady, while honoured with her approbation, I will support my claim against any man whatever.   205

SIR ANTHONY

Well said, Jack, and I'll stand by you, my boy.

---

182   *honour* for, humour (moodiness), or Mrs Malaprop may mean 'let's not have fighting simply to satisfy the sense of honour in front of the ladies'
183   *intimidate* terrify
186   *delusions* for, allusions
201   *support* back up (by fighting)

ACRES

Mind, I give up all my claim. I make no pretensions to anything in the world, and if I can't get a wife without fighting for her, by my valour, I'll live a bachelor.

SIR LUCIUS

Captain, give me your hand. An affront handsomely   210
acknowledged becomes an obligation. And, as for the lady, if she chooses to deny her own handwriting here –   (*Tak[es] out letters*)

MRS MALAPROP

O, he will dissolve my mystery! Sir Lucius, perhaps there's some mistake. Perhaps I can illuminate –   215

SIR LUCIUS

Pray, old gentlewoman, don't interfere where you have no business. Miss Languish, are you my Delia, or not?

LYDIA

Indeed, Sir Lucius, I am not.

LYDIA *and* ABSOLUTE *walk aside*

MRS MALAPROP

Sir Lucius O'Trigger, ungrateful as you are, I own the soft impeachment. Pardon my blushes – I am Delia.   220

SIR LUCIUS

You Delia? Foh, foh, be easy.

MRS MALAPROP

Why, thou barbarous Van Dyke, those letters are mine. When you are more sensible of my benignity, perhaps I may be brought to encourage your addresses.

SIR LUCIUS

Mrs Malaprop, I am extremely sensible of your   225
condescension; and whether you or Lucy have put this trick upon me, I am equally beholden to you. And to show you I'm not ungrateful, Captain Absolute, since you have taken that lady from me, I'll give you my Delia into the bargain.   230

214   *dissolve* for, solve or resolve
219–20   *soft impeachment* gentle accusation
222   *Van Dyke* the portrait painter Anthony Van Dyke (1599–1641); for, vandal
223   *sensible of my benignity* conscious of my kindness

ABSOLUTE

> I am much obliged to you, Sir Lucius; but here's our
> friend, Fighting Bob, unprovided for.

SIR LUCIUS

> Ha, little valour! Here, will you make your fortune?

ACRES

> Od's wrinkles! No! But give me your hand, Sir Lucius,
> forget and forgive. But if ever I give you a chance of   235
> *pickling* me again, say Bob Acres is a dunce, that's all.

SIR ANTHONY

> Come, Mrs Malaprop, don't be cast down. You are in
> your bloom yet.

MRS MALAPROP

> O Sir Anthony! Men are all barbarians.

> [SIR LUCIUS, ACRES, ABSOLUTE, SIR ANTHONY,
> DAVID, MRS MALAPROP, LYDIA] *retire
> leaving* JULIA *and* FAULKLAND

JULIA

> [*Aside*] He seems dejected and unhappy, not sullen. There   240
> was some foundation, however, for the tale he told me. O
> woman, how true should be your judgment, when your
> resolution is so weak!

FAULKLAND

> Julia, how can I sue for what I so little deserve? I dare
> not presume; yet hope is the child of penitence.   245

JULIA

> O Faulkland, you have not been more faulty in your
> unkind treatment of me, than I am now in wanting
> inclination to resent it. As my heart honestly bids me
> place my weakness to the account of love, I should be
> ungenerous not to admit the same plea for yours.   250

FAULKLAND

> Now I shall be blest indeed!

234   *me* 76 (us 75)
239   s.d. ed. (*All retire but* 75, 76)

SIR ANTHONY *comes forward*

SIR ANTHONY

What's going on here? So, you have been quarrelling too,
I warrant. Come, Julia, I never interfered before, but let
me have a hand in the matter at last. All the faults I have
ever seen in my friend Faulkland seemed to proceed   255
from what he calls the *delicacy* and *warmth* of his
affection for you. There, marry him directly, Julia, you'll
find he'll mend surprisingly!

([SIR LUCIUS, ACRES, ABSOLUTE, DAVID, MRS
MALAPROP, LYDIA] *come forward*)

SIR LUCIUS

Come now, I hope there is no dissatisfied person but
what is content; for as I have been disappointed myself, it   260
will be very hard if I have not the satisfaction of seeing
other people succeed better.

ACRES

You are right, Sir Lucius. So, Jack, I wish you joy.
Mr Faulkland the same. Ladies, come now, to show you I'm
neither vexed nor angry – od's tabors and pipes! – I'll   265
order the fiddles in half an hour to the New Rooms, and
I insist on your all meeting me there.

SIR ANTHONY

Gad, sir, I like your spirit; and at night we single lads
will drink a health to the young couples, and a husband to
Mrs Malaprop.   270

FAULKLAND

Our partners are stolen from us, Jack – I hope, to be
congratulated by each other. Yours, for having checked in
time the errors of an ill-directed imagination, which
might have betrayed an innocent heart; and mine, for
having, by her gentleness and candour, reformed the   275
unhappy temper of one, who by it made wretched whom
he loved most, and tortured the heart he ought to have
adored.

258   s.d. ed. (*The rest* 75, 76)
266   *New Rooms* situated in the Upper Town, near the Circus; they had been opened in 1771
267   *your* 76 (you 75)

ABSOLUTE

Well, Faulkland, we have both tasted the bitters, as well as
the sweets, of love – with this difference only: that *you*   280
always prepared the bitter cup for yourself, while *I* –

LYDIA

Was always obliged to *me* for it, hey, Mr Modesty? But
come, no more of that. Our happiness is now as
unallayed as general.

JULIA

Then let us study to preserve it so; and while hope   285
pictures to us a flattering scene of future bliss, let us
deny its pencil those colours which are too bright to be
lasting. When hearts deserving happiness would unite
their fortunes, virtue would crown them with an unfading
garland of modest, hurtless flowers; but ill-judging   290
passion will force the gaudier rose into the wreath,
whose thorn offends them, when its leaves are dropt!

[*Exeunt*]

Finis

279 *Faulkland* Larpent (Jack 75, 76) Every edition after Larpent has 'Jack' here, though
     Faulkland is clearly intended. Could it be that, in this play of telling doubles, Faulkland
     and Absolute have the same first name?
289 *fortunes* 76 (fortune 75)

EPILOGUE

BY THE AUTHOR

Spoken by Mrs Bulkley

Ladies, for *you*, I heard our poet say
He'd try to coax some *moral* from his play.
'One moral's plain', cried I, without more fuss,
'Man's social happiness all rests on us.
Through all the drama, whether damned or not,   5
Love gilds the *scene*, and *women* guide the *plot*.
From every rank obedience is our due.
D'ye doubt? The world's great stage shall prove it true.'

The cit, well skilled to shun domestic strife,
Will sup abroad; but, first, he'll ask his *wife*;   10
John Trot, his friend, for once will do the same,
But then he'll just *step home to tell my dame*.

The *surly squire* at noon resolves to rule,
And half the day 'Zounds! Madam is a fool!'
Convinced at night, the vanquished victor says,   15
'Ah, Kate! *You women have such coaxing ways*!'

The *jolly toper* chides each tardy blade,
Till reeling Bacchus calls on love for aid:
Then with each toast, he sees fair bumpers swim,
And kisses Chloe on the sparkling brim!   20

---

1 *our poet* the playwright
5 *damned* hissed in first performance
9 *the cit* the citizen
11 *John Trot* proverbial name for a stupid or ill-bred man
15 *vanquished victor* an allusion to John Dryden, *Alexander's Feast*, 1. 97: 'At length with love
   and win at once opprest / The vanquish'd victor sunk upon her breast'.
17 *toper* hard drinker
   chides each tardy blade tells off each slow-drinker
18 *Bacchus* god of wine in classical mythology
20 *Chloe* conventional name for a mistress in love poetry

[170]

Nay, I have heard that statesmen great and wise
Will *sometimes* counsel with a lady's eyes;
The servile suitors watch her various face,
She smiles preferment or she frowns disgrace,
Curtsies a pension here; there nods a place.   25

Nor with less awe, in scenes of humbler life,
Is *viewed* the *mistress*, or is *heard* the *wife*.
The poorest peasant of the poorest soil,
The child of poverty, and heir to toil,
Early from radiant love's impartial light,   30
Steals one small spark, to cheer his world of night:
Dear spark, that oft through winter's chilling woes,
Is all the warmth his little cottage knows!

The wand'ring *tar* who, not for *years*, has pressed
The widowed partner of his *day* of rest,   35
On the cold deck far from her arms removed
Still hums the ditty which his Susan loved:
And while around the cadence rude is blown,
The boatswain whistles in a softer tone.

The *soldier*, fairly proud of wounds and toil,   40
Pants for the *triumph* of his Nancy's smile;
But, ere the battle, should he list her cries,
The lover trembles and the hero dies!
That heart, by war and honour steeled to fear,
Droops on a sigh, and sickens at a tear!   45

But ye more cautious ye nice judging few,
Who give to beauty only beauty's due,
Though friends to love, *ye* view with deep regret
Our conquests marred, and triumphs incomplete,
'Till polished wit more lasting charms disclose,   50

22 *counsel with a lady's eyes* either 'converse with' or 'take advice from'
34 *tar* sailor
40 *fairly* rightly
42 *list* listen to
49 *and* 76 (*our* 75)

And judgment fix the darts which beauty throws!
In female breasts did sense and merit rule,
The lover's mind would ask no other school;
Shamed into sense the scholars of our eyes,
Our beaux from *gallantry* would soon be wise;   55
Would gladly light, their homage to improve,
The lamp of knowledge at the torch of love!

55   *beaux* fine gentlemen, lovers, dandies

APPENDIX

In the Larpent manuscript (see Textual Note) *The Rivals* has a different conclusion – and one that explains the title of the play. In III.v Sir Lucius dictates the wording of the challenge Acres is to make. Left alone, Acres writes out the challenge and, on David's advice, signs it with his 'love name', Colin, and addresses it to 'the lover of Miss Languish!' As a result, in this later scene, David delivers the challenge back to Sir Lucius instead of to Jack Absolute.

Act IV, Scene v

Enter DAVID, *with the challenge in his hand*

DAVID

Ah! Mercy on me! I wish I was fairly quit of my charge! If I had not drank my two good quarts, I hadn't had bodily strength to go through with it. But now, what with the ale and my own resolution, I hope I shall behave as becomes a gentleman's footman. Ah, David! Foolish David! Thee   5 hadst many warnings of this bloody business before thee'd left Clod Hall. Ay. It wasn't for nothing the dun cow held up her tail so piteously in the five acre close! Then the night before we set out, wa'n't there a huge raven, near as big as the parson, sat croaking on the faggot pile. Ay!   10 Truly. Croak, croak, croak, she want, as much as to say 'David, have an eye to your master'. What will the folks say at home? How Phyllis will howl when she hears of it. Ah! Poor bitch! She little thinks what shooting her master's going after. And I warrant Old Crop, who has   15 carried him field and road these ten years, will curse the hour he was born. A murrain light on this wicked scrawl. 'Fore George, it don't look like another letter. It is, as I may say, a designing and malicious looking letter. I handle it as a girl of fifteen would a cocked pistol. Foh! How it smells of   20 gunpowder. Oons! It may go off for what I know. I am marvellously tempted to lose it. I see no one watching by the house. Not I. Oons. Who comes here?

17 *murrain* a pestilence or plague usually affecting domestic animals

LUCY crosses the stage

'Tis only a woman. By the mass, 'tis Mrs Lucy.

Enter SIR LUCIUS *calling after* LUCY.
LUCY *returns. They talk together*

By the mass: that's he. Ay, that is certainly he. What a   25
height! Oons, he'll make no more of my master than I
should of a tame rabbit if it provoked me.

SIR LUCIUS
(*To* LUCY) Do so, and tell her I will be here tonight,
as soon as I have put the gentleman to death.

Exit LUCY

DAVID
O my poor master! I'll be rid of this, however, and do as I   30
was bid. (*Goes up to* SIR LUCIUS) No offence, sir, but
my master is a desperate fellow – with your leave, a
determined dog!

SIR LUCIUS
Your master!

DAVID
Ay, sir! Under favour he bid me tell you he was in a cruel   35
rage. With submission, sir, a most devouring rage.

SIR LUCIUS
Indeed! So this is some message from the Captain I
suppose. Well? What of his rage?

DAVID
There, sir, (*Giving him the letter*) no offence, I hope. 'Tis
none of my doing. A plague on them that put it in his head,   40
I say. I am only David, my poor master's servant. That is
till six o'clock, with your leave, sir. O, my poor master!   *Exit*

SIR LUCIUS
(*Reads*) 'To the lover of Miss Languish!' Ay, that's me
indeed. 'Confusion might arise . . . Expect . . . honour of
your company . . . Kingsmead Fields . . . six o'clock . . . shall   45
bring a friend . . . your Colin'. What the devil's Colin?
Well, if he don't choose to put his name, that's his
business. So, I find the form of these martial *billet-doux* is

48   *billet-doux* love letters – here used ironically

pretty much the same with everybody. I see he has
discovered my reason for quarrelling with him and chooses   50
to meet a little earlier. Well, faith, we shall be two and two,
and a very pretty quartetto we may make of it. He need not
have been afraid of my memory, however, for, upon my
conscience, I think a man who is not punctual in matters
of this kind never deserves to have an engagement while   55
he lives.   *Exit*

In this, the latter half of the concluding scene, Acres, Absolute and O'Trigger
realise that they are all rivals.

Act V, Scene iii

Enter SIR ANTHONY ABSOLUTE, DAVID, *and the*
CONSTABLES

SIR ANTHONY
What, points to points! Here, David, pull, you dog!

DAVID
Knock 'em all down, sweet constables. Knock down my
master in particular (*Draws* SIR ANTHONY's *sword,
and gives it him*), and bind his hands over to their good
behaviour!   5

SIR ANTHONY
Now in among 'em.

SIR LUCIUS
Pray, old gentleman, be easy! Don't you see we are four
already?

SIR ANTHONY
Put up, Jack, put up, or I shall be in a frenzy. How came
you in a duel, sir?   10

ABSOLUTE
Faith, sir, that's more than I can explain to you. Perhaps
that gentleman can tell you; 'twas he called on me, and
you know, sir, I serve his majesty.

SIR ANTHONY
Here's a pretty fellow; I catch him going to cut a man's
throat, and he tells me, he serves his majesty! Zounds,   15

3 s.d. *Draws* (*David draws* Larpent)

sirrah, then how durst you draw the king's sword against one of his subjects?

SIR LUCIUS

I called on the Captain, 'tis true, and he has given me his promise under his hand here to settle our difference. So if he wants to break his word –   20

SIR ANTHONY

Let me see! (*Takes the letter*)

ABSOLUTE

[*To* SIR LUCIUS] We shall meet when old ginger's out of the way.

SIR ANTHONY

Od's life! This isn't Jack's writing! (*Reads*) 'Prevent confusion . . . Kingsmead Fields . . . yours, Colin'. Zounds,   25
who's Colin?

ACRES

Od's triggers and flints! My fighting name! Why, Sir Anthony, let me see. [*Takes the letter*] By my valour, this is my challenge!

SIR LUCIUS

Your challenge!   30

SIR ANTHONY

So then you and Sir Lucius must fight!

ACRES

Od's blades, Sir Anthony, I should never have penned such a thing, if it had not been for Sir Lucius himself. Ask David else.

DAVID

Sir, my master is a peaceable master. By the mass, he   35
wouldn't challenge a worm, look'ee, of his own head.

ACRES

Besides, Sir Anthony, it is all Sir Lucius's inditing. Every word of it is his own.

SIR LUCIUS

I did indite it, I confess.

---

22 *old ginger* presumably Sir Anthony has ginger hair (the term 'ginger' meaning spirited is twentieth-century)

36 *worm . . . of his own head* conflation of 'wouldn't hurt a worm' and 'wouldn't hurt a hair of his head'

37 *inditing* composing

SIR ANTHONY

Gad's life, Sir Lucius, then you have challenged yourself.   40

SIR LUCIUS

Challenged myself! Hell and fury, sir, what do you mean? 'Sblood! I would resent an affront from myself as soon as from another gentleman. And if my honour were concerned in it, my right hand should measure swords with my left! How dare you laugh, gentlemen. But, look'ee, Mr Colin,   45 you shall answer for this! I see your tricks, and let me tell you that none but a rascal –

ACRES

Observe, gentleman, he calls me 'rascal'. 'Rascal' was the word, by my valour.

SIR LUCIUS

Well, sir?   50

ACRES

Look'ee, Sir Lucius, I don't mind 'rascal'. 'Rascal' may be said in a joke. But if you had said 'scoundrel', od's daggers and balls –

SIR LUCIUS

Well, sir?

ACRES

I should have thought you very ill bred.   55

SIR LUCIUS

Foh! You're beneath my notice. Observe me, gentlemen. Notwithstanding all this, there is a certain quality of affront given somewhere which must be expiated. We must fight – for it appears to me that we are all rivals.

ABSOLUTE

Explain your pretensions, Sir Lucius.   60

SIR LUCIUS

My pretensions are to the person and fortune of Miss Lydia Languish, and I'll cut any man's throat that stands in my way.

ABSOLUTE

A very concise method of wooing that.

ACRES

Out on her for a witch: I hate her. I make no pretensions to   65 anything in the world. And if I can't get a wife without fighting for her – by my valour, I'll live a bachelor!

44   *measure swords* ascertain that swords are of equal length – the preliminary to fighting a duel

ABSOLUTE

But on what do you ground your hopes?

SIR LUCIUS

On her affection for me, my dear – I only have it under
her own hand, that's all.   70

ABSOLUTE

Well, Sir Lucius, if that be the case, and the lady is willing
to ratify, I give you my honour, I will be no impediment.

SIR LUCIUS

Well, that's very fair.

SIR ANTHONY

What the deuce is all this? So, here comes the women. We
only wanted them to make the confusion complete.   75

Enter MRS MALAPROP, LYDIA [LANGUISH], JULIA
[MELVILLE], LUCY, *and* FAG

MRS MALAPROP

O, Sir Anthony! Tell us who's dead. O mercy! I am glad
to see you all horizontal on your legs. We have been led
such a dance.

SIR ANTHONY

We are all alive, I believe, Mrs Malaprop.

ACRES

Ay, thanks to my discretion.   80

MRS MALAPROP

Captain Absolute, come here. How could you intimidate us
so? Here's Lydia has been trembling like a gasping leaf for
you.

ABSOLUTE

For fear I should be killed, or escape, ma'am?

MRS MALAPROP

Come, come, no delusions to the past. Lydia is convinced.   85
Speak, Lydia.

SIR LUCIUS

With your leave, ma'am, I must put in a word here. You
know our agreement, Captain. I believe I could interpret the
young lady's silence. Now mark –

LYDIA

What is it you mean, sir?   90

77 *horizontal* for, vertical
82 *gasping* for, aspen

[178]

SIR LUCIUS

Come, come, Delia, we must be serious now; this is no
time for trifling.

LYDIA

'Tis true, sir; and your reproof bids me frankly offer this
gentleman my hand, and solicit the return of his
affections.   95

ABSOLUTE

O, my little angel, say you so?

SIR LUCIUS

What's this! Is this your promise that your love should
'never be miscellaneous'? Come out then, little Delia.

MRS MALAPROP

What can he mean? Sir Lucius, perhaps there is some
mistake. Perhaps I can illuminate –   100

SIR LUCIUS

Now pray, old gentlewoman, don't interfere where you
have no business. Miss Languish, are you my Delia or not?

LYDIA

Upon my word, Sir Lucius, I am not.

ABSOLUTE

Gad, Sir Lucius, here you have been challenging yourself –
are you sure you have not been making love to yourself?   105

SIR LUCIUS

'Sdeath, sir, how durst you –

ACRES

Ha, ha! Od's bulls and blunders! Jack, you have hit it – as
sure as can be, Sir Lucius is Delia himself.

SIR LUCIUS

Hark'ee, little valour, you'd best not provoke me. (To
LUCY) But come here, my queen of pins. Explain, my   110
little carrier, explain.

MRS MALAPROP

O he will perforate my mystery. Sir Lucius, ungrateful as
you are, I own the soft impeachment. Pardon my
chameleon blushes, I am Delia.

98 *miscellaneous* refers back to a line in Mrs Malaprop's letter to Sir Lucius, revised out of
    the 76 text, II.ii.33: 'As my motive is interested, you may be assured my love shall never
    be miscellaneous'. (Presumably) for, misallied, misapplied, erroneous or promiscuous.
112 *perforate* for, permeate
114 *chameleon* arboreal Old World lizard with the ability to change the colour of its skin; for,
    vermilion

SIR LUCIUS

You Delia? Foh, foh, be easy.   115

MRS MALAPROP

Come here, thou barbarous Van Dyke. Thou inhuman goat,
let me convict you.

(*Takes him aside*)

SIR ANTHONY

Well done, Aunt. So, to her Jack. Set matters right, and I'll
forgive you all.

(ABSOLUTE *and* LYDIA *walk aside*)

JULIA

[*Aside*] He seems dejected and unhappy, not sullen. There   120
was some foundation, however, for the tale he told me.
O woman, how true should be your judgment, when your
resolution is so weak!

FAULKLAND

Julia, how can I sue for what I so little deserve? I dare
not presume; yet hope is the child of penitence.   125

JULIA

O Faulkland, you have not been more faulty in your
unkind treatment of me, than I am now in wanting
inclination to resent it. As my heart honestly bids me
place my weakness to the account of love, I should be
ungenerous not to admit the same plea for yours.   130

[SIR ANTHONY *comes forward*]

SIR ANTHONY

What's going on here? So, what – you have been
quarrelling too, I warrant. Come, Julia, I never interfered
before, but let me have a hand in the matter at last. This
Faulkland is a very honest, odd, sensible, whimsical,
good-for-nothing kind of a fellow – and you are very fond   135
of him. So mind me, Julia! All the faults I have ever seen
in him seemed to proceed from what he calls the violence
and delicacy of his affection for you. There, marry him
directly, you'll find he'll mend surprisingly! So get along,

116   *thou* 75, 76 (tho', Larpent)
117   *convict* for, convince

fix the day, and let Dean Hymen have but one trouble with   140
you all. Why, Mr Acres, you and I are left here like single
birds in pairing time.

ACRES

Od's life! No, here's David, and –

DAVID

Ay, here's David.

ACRES

– and yonder's a couple that don't seem quite agreed.   145

SIR ANTHONY

What Fag. You dog! Ah, you've been a sad scoundrel, Fag.

FAG

Sir, you are pleased to be partial. I have had the best of
masters.

SIR ANTHONY

A very sad dog indeed, Fag. What, you are trying to delude
poor simple Lucy? You want to marry too, hey?   150

FAG

Marry! O lud, no, sir! One married couple in a family will
be quite enough. Not that I have ever entertained any
vulgar prejudices against the state – but we were both
rather too keen blades before. And if we were riveted in
matrimony, we shall cut like a pair of scissors.   155

(FAULKLAND, JULIA, ABSOLUTE *and* LYDIA *come forward*)

SIR LUCIUS

Come now, I hope there is no dissatisfied person but what
is content. Captain Absolute, I ask your pardon for the
trouble I have given you; Mrs Malaprop has very agreeably
convinced me of my error! We were only rivals by mistake.
And Mr Acres too, my other rival that was, I must beg your   160
pardon for – unless you make pretensions to this lady also?

ACRES

Od's wrinkles, no! Give me your hand, Sir Lucius, say no
more, forget and forgive. But if I ever give you a chance of
pickling me again, say Bob Acres is a dunce, that's all. So,
Jack, I wish you joy. Mr Faulkland the same to you. Ladies,   165
come now, to show you I am neither vexed nor angry –

---

140 *Hymen* the Greek god of marriage

od's tabors and pipes! – I'll order the fiddles in half an hour to the New Rooms, and I insist on your all meeting me there.

ABSOLUTE

Well said, Bob! So now our happiness is general, and we shall laugh without hurting anyone.   170

SIR ANTHONY

Od's life, here's all the town staring at us. All's public, as sure as can be. Zounds, the field is as crowded as a playhouse the first night of a new comedy.

ACRES

The more the merrier! I'll invite all I can to be of our party. And at supper we single lads, Sir Anthony, will drink a   175 good voyage to you young ones – hey, Mrs Malaprop!

FAULKLAND

Jack, our partners are stolen from us – I hope, to be congratulated by each other. Yours, for having checked in time the errors of an ill-directed imagination, which might have betrayed an innocent heart; and mine, for   180 having, by her gentleness and candour, reformed the unhappy temper of one, who, by it, made wretched whom he loved most, and tortured the heart he ought to have adored.

ABSOLUTE

Well, Faulkland, we have both tasted the bitters, as well as   185 the sweets, of love – with this difference only: that *you* have always prepared the bitter cup for yourself, while *I* –

LYDIA

Was always obliged to *me* for it, hey, Mr Modesty?

JULIA

It is a common observation, the evils of love are more numerous than its blessings – but I believe the former was   190 mostly of our own creating. When hearts deserving happiness would unite their fortunes, virtue would crown them with an unfading garland of modest, hurtless flowers; but ill-judging passion will force the gaudier rose into the wreath, whose thorn offends them, when its leaves are   195 dropt!

[*Exeunt*]